OLD TESTAMENT CHALLENGE 3

DEVELOPING A HEART FOR GOD

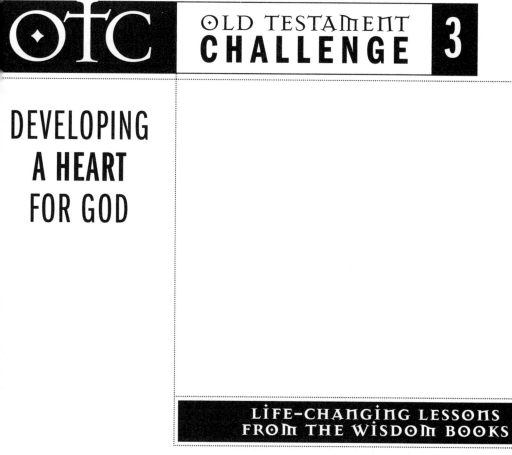

OTC OLD TESTAMENT CHALLENGE 3

DEVELOPING
A HEART
FOR GOD

LIFE-CHANGING LESSONS
FROM THE WISDOM BOOKS

JOHN ORTBERG
WITH KEVIN & SHERRY HARNEY

ZONDERVAN™

GRAND RAPIDS, MICHIGAN 49530 USA

WILLOW
Willow Creek Resources

ZONDERVAN™

Old Testament Challenge: Developing a Heart for God — Discussion Guide
Copyright © 2003 by Willow Creek Association

Requests for information should be addressed to:
Zondervan, *Grand Rapids, Michigan 49530*

ISBN 0-310-25033-1

Interior design by Sharon VanLoozenoord

Interior composition by Tracey Moran

Printed in the United States of America

03 04 05 06 07 08 09 /❖ DC/ 10 9 8 7 6 5 4 3 2 1

Contents

OTC

İntroduction

There are some things in this life that always seem to be in high demand but short supply. Wisdom is one of them. In our fast-paced world of sound bites and canned answers, we need a source of deep wisdom that does not change with each new fad and trend. The wisdom books of the Old Testament offer a fountain of truth to quench our thirsting hearts and refresh our parched souls.

These eight small group sessions will introduce you to some of the core themes found in the wisdom literature.

- David's example of a heart that longs for God will become a model for us to follow as we grow in intimacy with our heavenly Father.
- The Psalms will become our prayer book as we discover that God invites us to speak to him when we are filled with praise but also when we are facing deep sorrow.
- Various kinds of prayer, ranging from lament to confession to thanksgiving, will come alive as we learn from the honest words of the psalmists.
- Hearts will race as we look at the romance and passion of the Song of Songs.
- The contemporary relevance of the book of Proverbs will come alive as we learn how to flee from folly and grow in wisdom.
- The book of Job will give us insight into the heart of God as well as help us learn how to face hard times.
- Finally, the heart-breaking civil war and subsequent division of Israel will help us see how God continues to work among his people even when they resist his leading.

The wisdom books reveal the heart of God. He is intent on loving us as his children even when we run from him. God also longs for us as his followers to grow in our ability to love him, and others, with all our hearts. But how do we learn to love God with passion and consistency? Where can we find the practical tools to develop a heart for God?

OTC

This small group study will lead you through the wisdom books of the Old Testament and unveil truths that will help you grow in your love for God and others. This literature will take you on a journey from the heights of joyful romance to the depths of human loss and sorrow and reveal the pathway to loving God each step of the way. In a world where wisdom is in short supply, these books of the Bible offer a storehouse of the wisdom we all need so desperately.

David: Developing a Heart for God

2 SAMUEL 6:1-22; 11:1-17; 12:1-9

Introduction

It is in the desert that David was at his best. That's where his life was shaped and defined by God. David experienced many victories in battle. He had accomplishments, wealth, and the praise of people. But when it was all said and done, David seemed to be at his best when he was in the furnace of the desert. The dry air would crack his lips; the heat would drain his energy; but in this arid place of desolate silence, David met with God. In the desert he wrote many of the psalms, he spoke to God, and he learned.

Rarely do God's people ask to be placed in the desert. It would seem masochistic to ask God for such an experience. Yet God often led his people to this place of training, discipline, refining, and preparation. Moses spent time in the desert, and so did the nation of Israel. David was trained in the desert-school. Even Jesus, who never sinned, was led by the Spirit into the desert for forty days.

Sometimes God leads those he loves through a season of desert wandering. But when he does this, it is always with a purpose. When we find ourselves in the desert, we need to look to God and ask, "What can I learn in this place?" We need to avoid the natural reaction of running away. We need to learn, as David did, that God does some of his best work when we are in the desert.

Looking at Life

Tell about a desert experience you have faced and how God strengthened you and changed you through it. How would our lives be different if we never faced wilderness times?

1

Learning from the Word
Read: 2 Samuel 6:1-22

CELEBRATING GOD!

The ark of the covenant was the closest thing Israel had to a throne for God. Over the mercy seat, on the ark, the presence of God was said to dwell. It was a sacred reminder to Israel that God was with them. David knew that the ark belonged in Jerusalem. As a result, he got a group together and went down to get the ark from the house of Abinadab. Just to give you a sense of how important this was to David, he chose thirty thousand men to accompany him to retrieve the ark. After a long journey getting the ark back to Jerusalem, an incredible party broke out.

Picture Mardi Gras, the Rose Parade, and New Year's Eve in Time Square all rolled into one! The celebration that accompanied the return of the ark was huge! God's presence could be felt and seen. A party erupted and rolled through Jerusalem. In a public setting, David was swept into worship. With all his might he began to express his praise and thanks to God. It was full body, full contact, no-holds-barred worship.

2

Imagine you were a citizen in Jerusalem when David came in dancing before the ark with all his might. How do you think you would have responded?

What might some of the conversations around dinner tables in Jerusalem have sounded like that night?

3

What keeps you from expressing yourself with passionate abandon in worship?

What helps you express yourself freely in worship?

4

Read: 2 Samuel 11:1–17

TEMPTATION: WHO IS ON THE THRONE?

David notices Bathsheba, a beautiful woman, bathing a couple of rooftops over from the palace. He sends his servants to bring her to the palace. David is clearly warned that she is the wife of Uriah the Hittite. It is important to know that Uriah was one of David's most faithful warriors. He is named among David's legendary thirty mighty men (1 Chronicles 11:41). He was with David during his desert years and had served the king and fought at his side.

Knowing all of this, David still brings her to the palace and sleeps with her. In one moment of temptation and weakness, David changes the course of his life. This one choice set off a chain reaction that led to coveting, adultery, lying, and murder, and it even cost the lives of some innocent soldiers in David's army!

As you read this story of David's temptation and the various sinful actions that followed, at what points along the way could he have stopped this downward spiral?

5

As you read the story of David's fall into sin, how do you see one sin leading to another in a domino effect?

6 It has been said that three of the greatest potential areas we can fall into sin are:

- Areas we have sinned in the past
- Areas we believe we will never sin
- Areas of life where there is a pattern of sin in our family

Why is each of these areas a point of potential temptation in our lives?

7 When you feel temptation setting in, what helps you say "no" and resist temptation?

> It is not temptation itself that grieves God; he is displeased when we give in to temptation.
> —CHARLES STANLEY

Read: 2 Samuel 12:1–9

THE MINISTRY OF NATHAN

Nathan had the courage to speak the truth. As king, David could have spoken one word and had Nathan executed. Nathan's willingness to go face-to-face with the king and confront him with his sin was no small thing. This step was bold and risky.

Nathan was ready to call sin exactly what it was. He did this because he spoke for God and God never sugar coats sin. Nathan's job was to call David to a higher standard—God's standard. Because of his ministry, David's heart finally broke over his sin. He came to a place of humble confession and repentance. The ministry of Nathan was the call to speak the truth with loving boldness. It was a hard ministry because it put relationships at risk. But it is a ministry we all need to be ready to receive when God sends a Nathan to call us to repentance and humble confession.

At the end of David's life, when it was all said and done, how do you think each of these people would respond to this statement: "Sin is no big deal! I can do what I want and it won't impact others or hurt me!"

- David
- Bathsheba
- Nathan
- God
- Uzziah
- The unnamed child of their infidelity

8

> Sin will always take you farther than you want to go, cost you more than you want to pay, and keep you longer than you want to stay.
>
> —AUTHOR UNKNOWN

Nathan became God's tool to help David see sin in his life and to lovingly bring him to a place of humble repentance. Why is it important to have a "Nathan" in our lives?

9

Who is a "Nathan" in your life, and why do you appreciate this person?

Sometimes, when a person falls into temptation and gets caught in a pattern of sin, others look on from the sidelines and say, "I saw that coming!" They knew what was going on, but never spoke a word of warning! What keeps us from speaking up when we see sin and potential danger creeping into the life of another follower of Christ?

10

Closing Reflection

Take a few minutes of silence for personal reflection . . .

As a follower of Christ, take time to invite God to be the only one on the throne of your heart. Become honest. Confess where other things have taken God's place on the throne and invite God to rule and reign in every area of your life.

Take time to respond to these closing questions:

We are all tempted to let people and things crowd God off the throne. It can be a person who has become more important to us than God. It can be a hobby, sport, or personal interest that capitalizes on our time and becomes our first love. It can be a habit we know is self-destructive, but we just can't seem to resist. If you had to identify one thing that is most prone to end up on the throne of your life (other than God), what is it?

What can you do to keep this off the throne, and how can your small group members pray for you in this area of your life?

Close your small group by praying together . . .

Sin is deceitful and our hearts are skilled at ignoring it. Yet, God wants to lead us to a place of seeing, admitting, and confessing our sin. This process can't begin until we identify the places of hidden sin in our lives. Psalm 139:23–24 says:

> *Search me, O God, and know my heart;*
> *test me and know my anxious thoughts.*
> *See if there is any offensive way in me.*

Close your small group with a time of praying for God to:

- Search your hearts
- Uncover hidden sin
- Give strength to go in the way everlasting

Old Testament Life Challenge
Getting Undignified

David tried to worship God with all his might. What would it look like if you took some steps forward as a worshiper? What risks might you take?

Ask the Holy Spirit to fill your heart and church in new and fresh ways. Pray about taking risks as his worshiper. Seek to let your outward expressions of worship be consistent with what is happening in your heart. Seek to worship in a way that is a natural and free expression of the activity of the Holy Spirit inside of you.

You may want to begin by singing praise with all your might when you are driving down the road, standing in the shower, or worshiping with God's people. Maybe you have wanted to lift your hands in worship for a long time but have always resisted because you fear what others might think. The next time you sense the Spirit prompting you to lift your hands, begin by simply turning them upward in your lap. Let your outward posture match what is happening in the depth of your heart. Begin taking steps of responsiveness to God's leading in worship.

The Heights and Depths of Prayer

PSALMS 42; 103; 136:1-4; 137:1-4

Introduction

The book of Psalms contains some of the most uplifting and encouraging words ever penned. At the same time, it contains some of the most honest and tearful prayers lifted up by God's people. The psalms range from the heights of joy to the depths of sorrow, and they contain every emotion between these two extremes.

Suppose you wake up one morning and decide to read Psalm 136:1–4. Here is what will greet you:

> Give thanks to the LORD, for he is good.
> > His love endures forever.
> Give thanks to the God of gods.
> > His love endures forever.
> Give thanks to the Lord of lords:
> > His love endures forever.
> to him who alone does great wonders,
> > His love endures forever.

If you want to have a good start to your day, this psalm is the ticket! It brings a positive feeling of celebration, victory, and joy. This is a psalm that will breathe life into your soul.

Suppose the next day you continue your reading and turn to Psalm 137:1–4. This is how your reading will begin:

> By the rivers of Babylon we sat and wept
> > when we remembered Zion.
> There on the poplars
> > we hung our harps,
> for there our captors asked us for songs,
> > our tormentors demanded songs of joy;
> > they said, "Sing us one of the songs of Zion!"
> How can we sing the songs of the LORD
> > while in a foreign land?

This psalm is sung in a minor key by people who are in exile. These are prisoners of war. Their hearts are broken and they are weeping. As you read this psalm you may find yourself saying, "Well, that's not very happy. That doesn't make me feel very good."

But here is the truth of the matter: It is not meant to make you feel good. It is there for you to learn to express your sorrow when you feel oppressed, abandoned, and alone. The beauty of the psalms is that they help us express our hearts no matter where we are in our journey of faith and no matter how we are feeling.

Looking at Life

1

Does Psalm 136 or Psalm 137 most accurately express how you are feeling today? Why does this psalm connect for you right now?

Learning from the Word
Read: Psalm 103

THE HEART OF WORSHIP

The heart of worship is to delight in the goodness, greatness, and glory of God. It is to reflect deeply on his character and attributes and then to respond in natural praise and adoration. We then express this directly to him, and we know he receives it. Worship is to reflect on God with our mind, our will, and our heart in a way that moves us to delight in him and then to be overwhelmed as we realize that he also delights in us, far more than we ever dreamed.

Worship involves all of who we are entering into intimate relationship with the God who made and loves us. William Temple said it like this:

> To worship is to quicken the conscience by the holiness of God, to feed the mind with the truth of God, to purge the imagination by the beauty of God, to open the heart to the love of God, to devote the will to the purpose of God.

2

In Psalm 103 David gives many reasons why we can lift up praise and worship to God. What is one reason David expresses that connects with where your heart is today, and why does this reason for praise resonate for you?

According to this psalm, *who* and *what* should lift up praise and worship to God?

3

How might each of these express this praise?

Sometimes things are going well. The sun is shining, relationships are running smoothly, there is money in the bank, and we have a sense of God's presence and favor. Why is it important that we lift up our prayers of celebration, joy, and praise at these times?

4

What might we miss if we fail to pray to God at these times?

5

Read: Psalm 42

PRAYERS FROM THE DEPTHS

The psalms of lament are radically different from the psalms of praise. These are recorded in the Bible to help us learn how to pray in our times of pain, sorrow, fear, and loss. Just as God welcomes our prayers of praise, he also gladly receives our prayers of lament.

Some people may think, *I don't think I know how to lament. I am not sure what a lament really is.* Here are four questions:

- Do you know how to complain?
- If your body is aching, do you know how to groan?
- When hard times come, do you ever shed tears of sorrow?
- When people treat you unfairly, do you ever tell God that you are hurting?

If you answered yes to any of these questions, you already know something about laments. A lament psalm is basically a complaint. It is an honest and heartfelt expression of pain, sadness, and brokenness. The psalms of lament are actually the largest single category in the whole book of Psalms.

These psalms deal with a number of areas of struggle, but they tend to be somewhat general. There are very few details in these psalms, and this is intentional on the part of the psalmists. These psalms were written to be all-purpose prayers. They can be used by people in many and various situations. The beauty of these psalms is that we can adapt them to our unique needs. We can use them to give voice to our own pain, struggle, and sorrow.

6 What is happening in the life of the psalmist and what is he facing that is causing him to lift up this prayer of lament (Psalm 42) to God?

7 In the psalms of lament there is often a strange mix of *honest lament* and *hopeful confidence* in God. How do you see these two themes woven together in this psalm?

8 Scholars have identified four primary areas of complaint that are common in the lament prayers found in psalms. They are:

- fear of enemies
- battles with illness
- the reality of death
- anxiety of being trapped

Tell about how you have faced *one* of these realities and how you have brought this before God in prayer.

What is one pain, sorrow, or fear you are facing in your life right now?

9

How can your small group members pray for you and support you as you face this?

> Trouble and perplexity
> drive me to prayer; and prayer drives
> away perplexity and trouble.
> —PHILIPP MELANCHTHON, SIXTEENTH CENTURY

AFFIRMATION OF PRAISE

Although the laments do have the feeling of a complaint, they are unique in that they almost always have a feeling of hope. Even in the deepest pits of despair, the psalmist seems to have an unquenchable spirit of hope. Bernhard W. Anderson, in his classic book *Out of the Depths (The Psalms Speak for Us Today)*, writes:

> The term "lament" is not an altogether satisfactory label for these psalms. The word may suggest a pessimistic view of life, a "bemoaning of a tragedy which cannot be reversed." But this is not the mood of the psalmists. What characterizes these psalms, with very few exceptions, is the confidence that the situation can be changed if Yahweh wills to intervene.

How have you experienced hope and strength during a time of deep sorrow or loss?

10

Closing Reflection

Take a few minutes of silence for personal reflection . . .

God wants us to meet with him in prayer, no matter what we are facing in our lives. Some people tend to come to him freely and naturally when things are going great. Prayers from the heights come easily for these people. Others come into God's presence naturally when they are in the depths. Lament is their most natural prayer. But God wants us to come to him when we are on the heights of joy and in the depths of sorrow. Do you tend to lift up prayers of praise or lament most naturally? Is there a kind of prayer that you tend to avoid? Which kind of prayer do you need to develop more in your life?

Take time to respond to these closing questions:

Do you need to develop the ability to lift up prayers of praise or prayers of lament?

What might help you grow in this kind of prayer expression?

Close your small group by praying together . . .

God sees us, right where we are, and he loves us. If you have a hard time accepting this truth, remember the words of Romans 5:8, "But God demonstrates his own love for us in this: While we were still sinners, Christ died for us." Sometimes we try to hide the truth about our lives from God. As ridiculous as this may sound, we actually try to keep God from seeing the mess in our lives. What we must do is invite God into the mess. He invites us to tell him about the fears we hold in our heart, the anger that we nurse, our hidden desires, and all the things we would rather not talk about.

Move in two directions as you close in prayer:

- Express your sorrow, pain, and prayers of lament to God.
- Lift up your prayer of hope and confidence in God, even in the midst of your struggles.

Old Testament Life Challenge
Calling Yourself to Worship

In Psalm 103:1–2 David calls himself to worship. In the morning we can echo David's prayer and say:

> Praise the LORD, O my soul;
>> all my inmost being, praise his holy name.
> Praise the LORD, O my soul,
>> and forget not all his benefits.

Then we can do exactly that, all day long.

We can call ourselves to worship when we are getting ready to gather with God's people. We tend to rush into church at the last minute. For some the only real consistent preparation is getting a cup of coffee into their system before the service starts. Why not get a good night of rest the day before worship as part of your personal preparation? You may want to make a point of arriving early so you can pray and prepare. You can use the drive time to pray silently or even out loud with others in the car. If you know the passage you will be studying as a congregation, why not read it in advance? Get creative in finding ways to call yourself to worship and prepare to meet with God.

The Greatest Prayers of All Times

PSALMS 30; 51; 96; 119:1-16

Introduction: Now I Lay Me Down to Sleep

How do you teach someone to pray? Jesus' disciples came to him and said, "Lord, teach us to pray." All followers of Christ desire authentic prayer experiences. But where do we look to find tools to develop our prayer lives?

Many parents have grappled with this question and have developed ways to teach their children to pray. Many children learn to pray by talking to God each night before bed. Often it looks something like this: First, kneel next to the bed, fold your hands, close your eyes, and say, "Now I lay me down to sleep, I pray thee, Lord, my soul to keep. If I should die before I wake, I pray thee, Lord, my soul to take. God bless. . . ." At this point the child lists as many people as come to mind, and they finish with a declarative "Amen!"

Is there anything wrong with this approach to teaching prayer? No. This is a wonderful prayer. It is a great *starting point* for children. It is also helpful to teach some basic prayers that can be offered before a meal or at a time of need. But if a Christian goes year after year and the entire sum of his or her prayer life is what he or she learned as a child, something is missing. There is so much more!

Looking at Life

If you received training in prayer as a child, what were you taught?

1

How was this training helpful, or hurtful, to your development as a person of prayer?

Learning from the Word
Read: Psalm 30

WHAT DO YOU SAY?

It is a short sentence, only two words. The entire declaration is only two syllables, but it is hard to learn. The sentence is, "Thank you!"

All parents discover that part of their job is to ask each child, over and over again, "What do you say?" When a meal is served, they ask their daughter, "Honey, what do you say?" When a gift is received from grandparents, they prompt their son, "Danny, what do you say?" When a neighbor has given them a ride home from school, they ask them, "What do you say?" Over and over, year after year, parents ask their children this question countless times in a variety of ways.

Why do parents do this? Because thanksgiving should be a natural response to the goodness and kindness we experience in this life. But, sadly, we often forget to express thankfulness. Parents ask this question again and again, longing for the day when their son or daughter will say it on his or her own. What joy fills a mother's heart when a son or daughter gives a smile and says, "Thanks, Mom!" all on his or her own.

2 In Psalm 30 David expresses thankfulness about many things and in many ways. What is David thankful for and how does he express it?

3 Without using a name, tell about a time when someone failed to express thanks when they should have done or said something to communicate deep gratitude.

How did you feel when you saw this lack of gratitude?

Worship—the only gift we can bring to God that he himself has not first given to us.

—ISOBEL RALSTON

What are some ways we can express thankfulness to God for all he has done for us?

4

Read: Psalm 51

THE LIFE-SAVING VALUE OF EXAMINATION

The book of Psalms contains prayers that are focused on the confession of sin. These are called penitential psalms. Such prayers function like X rays that look into us and show where we are broken and where the sickness of sin is hidden. We need these psalms for our souls in the same way we need a regular physical to be sure we are physically healthy.

When we visit a doctor and go through the standard battery of tests, the examination helps identify all kinds of potential problems. The exam does not hurt us, but it helps show possible dangers to our health. Prayers of confession function in the same way. When we come before God and invite his Spirit to examine our hearts, when we freely confess our weaknesses, and when we admit our need for God's forgiveness, we are on the road to spiritual health.

Psalm 51 was written by David after he had committed adultery with Bathsheba and had her husband killed to cover up his sin. Respond to *one* of the following questions about David in light of Psalm 51:

5

- How is David feeling about himself at the moment he writes this prayer?
- What is David's vision of God?
- What does David promise in this penitential prayer?
- What is the longing of David's heart?

6

When you come to a place of honest confession, how does this impact your ability to relate to God and to others?

Read: Psalm 119:1–16

WISDOM PSALMS

The wisdom psalms give instruction and guidance to God's people. They praise and celebrate God's law. They rejoice in the pure beauty of the words God has given us in the Scriptures. These psalms are geared to motivate and help us desire to follow the teachings of the Bible with all our heart. One of the most remarkable chapters in all the Bible is Psalm 119. This psalm has 176 verses, and every one of them celebrates the wonder of God's Word and calls us to delight in it.

7

There are many ways to enter into the wisdom psalms in our own prayer life. Choose *one* of the options below and write a brief prayer about God's Word:

- Thank God for his Word and the wisdom it offers.
- Ask God to help you grow in the knowledge of his Word.
- Celebrate the truth and power of God's Word.
- Cry out for the Holy Spirit to give you power to obey God's Word.
- Marvel in the wonder and beauty of the Scriptures.

Take time for group members to volunteer to read their prayer out loud. As a group, enter into this prayer and pray it for each other and for yourself.

Tell about your personal goals for study of God's Word. How can your small group members keep you accountable to be growing in God's Word?

8

Read: Psalm 96

REMEMBER WHO IS ON THE THRONE

We need to learn from the example of the people of God in the Old Testament. When times were hard, they kept their eyes on the one who rules and reigns. In the midst of sickness, in scarcity, in exile, under the oppression of the Assyrians or Babylonians, during the time when Jerusalem and the temple and all they loved were a distant memory, they turned to these psalms. Every time they read Psalm 96 and other enthronement psalms, they remembered, "Our God reigns."

When we go through the trials this life brings, when we are hurting and feeling powerless, we need to look to the throne of God and remember that he rules. Also, when we talk with other Christ followers who have lost their focus, we may need to point them back to the throne and remind them who is in charge of this universe.

In this psalm, the writer has his eyes fixed firmly on the throne of God. What does he see?

9

What response comes from the heart of the psalmist when he sees God enthroned in glory?

10

When we turn our eyes away from God's throne and focus on our troubles and life's struggles, how can this impact us?

What helps you keep your eyes focused on God in his splendor rather than your problems?

Closing Reflection

Take a few minutes of silence for personal reflection . . .

Which of the prayers comes most naturally in your life?

- Prayers of thanksgiving
- Prayers of confession
- Wisdom prayers
- Enthronement prayers

Which of these kinds of prayers is most difficult for you?

Take time to respond to these closing questions . . .

Which kind of prayer do you need to develop most in your life? What can you do to develop in this area of your prayer life?

Close your small group by praying together . . .

First, invite God to help in the process of searching your heart. Self-examination is only safe and right when we do it with God's help.

Second, come before God humbly and pray for the convicting ministry of the Holy Spirit to take place in your heart. If there is hidden sin or rebellion, confess it and ask for power to live a transformed life.

Old Testament Life Challenge

Remember to Say Thank You!

Just as children need to hear parents ask them, "What do you say?" we also need to be reminded to be thankful. The truth is, sometimes we forget. We get busy, we become selfish, or we just get used to God's goodness and don't notice how gracious he is to us.

Commit to grow as a person of thankfulness.

Daily reminders: Use the things that come up every day as thanksgiving prompters. Here are some ideas of things that can remind you to pause and lift up thanks to God:

- when you wake up in the morning
- each time you have a meal
- whenever you hear someone complain (including yourself!)
- each time you hear a bird chirp, a dog bark, or a cat meow
- when a baby cries
- when you hit a green light (and when you hit a red light)
- when someone smiles at you (and when someone scowls)
- when you lay your head on the pillow at the end of the day

Identify one specific thing that happens regularly in your day and use this as a thanksgiving prompter.

Life Application: Extending Forgiveness

Think about David for a moment. After he committed murder, adultery, and a number of other sins, his heart was broken, and he came back to the Lord (Psalm 51). He asked God for mercy and compassion. David pleaded with God to blot out his transgressions and wash away all his sin. David realized there was great brokenness in him and that he could not get himself out of the pit he had fallen into. Only God could save him. David also committed to help extend grace to others and turn them back to God.

Like David, when we have become aware of the greatness of God's grace toward us, we want to help others know that his grace is available to them as well. We can begin by seeking to have a forgiving heart toward those who have wronged us. The more we understand and accept the forgiveness God offers, the more freely we extend grace to those who have wronged us.

Enter the Romance

SONG OF SONGS

Introduction

When God created human beings, he made men and women. In the creation of Adam and Eve we see that God's plan included a man and a woman together in the community of covenant love. In Eden, before the Fall, God said, "Be fruitful and multiply." It is clear that human romance and sexual intimacy were part of God's perfect plan. Even in Paradise, before sin entered in, God saw his creation of a man and woman in intimate relationship and declared it, "Very good!"

The Song of Songs is a celebration of God's plan for romantic and sexual intimacy in the covenant of a marriage relationship. It is a bold reminder that God made us male and female and that his plan is still good. No matter how the world misuses God's good gifts, he always has the power and desire to restore them to his original plan.

There are those who teach that the Song of Songs is really an allegory of God's love for his people, the church. Generally people who hold this position have not read this book closely. There is no indication of that anywhere in the text.

Song of Songs starts right in with kissing in the very first section, and then it really gets going! It is a raw, unabashed, uninhibited celebration of romance and sexual attraction and passion between a man and a woman. Every indication, from looking at the text of this book, is that it is not an allegory about the church but an honest expression of love between two people.

THREE MOVEMENTS IN THE DRAMA

There are three primary movements in the Song of Songs. These help us follow the plotline of the book. They are:

Movement 1: Anticipation (1:1–3:5). As you read this section, you meet a couple who is crazy in love. They can't wait to be together. They long for each other. But they are not married yet, so they dream of, await, and prepare for that day.

Movement 2: The wedding and honeymoon (3:6–5:1). This section is a poetic, stylized description of a wedding. It's a picture of commitment and covenant, but it is highly stylized.

Movement 3: Their relationship after the wedding (romance and relationship) (5:2–8:14). The rest of the book is a celebration of love, romance, and the joy of covenantal sexual intimacy. It is a great reminder that while true romantic fulfillment begins on the wedding day, it does not end there.

Looking at Life

1

Song of Songs makes it clear that God is a big fan of romance and human sexuality—in fact, he invented them! Why do so many people think that God is opposed to passion and sexual expression?

MEETING THE CHARACTERS

There are three main characters in the Song of Songs:

The woman. She is often called "the beloved." This woman is deeply in love and longs for her lover. She is bold in her expressions of praise for his character. She also freely expresses her longing for intimacy and the depth of love she has for the man.

The man. He is called "the lover." This man is a common shepherd, but the woman sees him as if he were a king. He is also bold in his declaration of love and is quick to praise his beloved. He celebrates her beauty and rejoices in her love.

The friends of the woman. They speak in concert together. Their combined voice celebrates the relationship of the man and woman and cheers them on in their relationship.

As you read the Song of Songs, most Bibles have captions that tell who is speaking. These headings are not in the Hebrew text. They have been supplied by interpreters to help us understand who is speaking at each point in the story. Because this is a poetic book, these title headings help us stay in touch with the drama and movement of the book.

Learning from the Word
Read: Song of Songs 1; 4:1-7

THE DELIGHT FACTOR

There is a striking feature that runs through Song of Songs that might be called "the delight factor." Behind the words of this man and woman is a deep desire to build each other up. They go out of their way to celebrate the other person and take great delight in everything about her or him. They get quite creative in how they do this and in the words they use. Their words pour out of a generous heart. Each has a deep longing to build up the other and celebrate who he or she is.

The problem for the modern reader is that much of the imagery and words of delight don't translate well into our own language. Imagine a wife taking her husband to a mall to help her pick out a dress for a wedding they will be attending. She gathers a few options and heads into the dressing room. He sits in the special "husband-chair" strategically positioned just outside of the dressing room area. There he waits for the moment she reappears. He knows what the question will be, for he has sat in this chair before.

How do I look?

He pauses, reflects, and then he says, "You look like a horse!"

Let's be honest, this would not go over very well! In our day, calling a woman a horse would not be a complimentary thing. Some images just don't transfer over from the Song of Songs to the changing room of a major department store.

What are some of the delight-filled word pictures used in Song of Songs (chapter 1 and 4:1–7), and what do you think the man and woman are trying to say to each other?

2

What are some modern-day expressions of delight that might not make sense a hundred years from now?

3

Why are specific, vivid, and creative expressions of affirmation and celebration so important in a romantic relationship?

4

Many people have studied the language of love and discovered that people express love and receive it differently. Here are just three of the many ways love can be expressed and received. Which of these is most natural for you as you seek to communicate love and care for others and which of these do you most appreciate when others seek to communicate love and care to you?

- giving and receiving gifts or tokens of affection
- verbal affirmation and words of blessing
- physical expressions of tender intimacy

Why is knowing the love language of a spouse so critical for a healthy relationship?

Read: Song of Songs 4:16–5:1

THE ROLE OF FRIENDS

The friends in this scene are giving a toast to the bride and groom and cheering for their intimacy and closeness. There is a specific role that the friends play in this book of the Bible. They cheer, bless, and give positive direction to the couple. This is still the role of those who have friends who are married.

Marriages don't occur in vacuums. When we think about friends who are married, we should ask the question, "Is their marriage stronger and better because of me?" We can all learn more about how we can encourage and bless those who are married.

5

Why is it so important for a married couple to have a chorus of friends who bless them and build them up in their marriage?

Think of a married couple you know and care about. You are in their chorus of friends. What can you say and do to build up this couple and help strengthen their marriage?

6

If you are married, take a moment to think about who is in your chorus of friends who affirm your married life and encourage you to build a marriage that pleases God. How is God using these people to bring stability and fortification to your marriage?

7

What could you do to express thankfulness to these people for what they mean to you and your spouse?

Read: Song of Songs 5:1–8; 8:6–7

THE STORY GOES ON

The wedding day is not the end, it is the beginning. Too many couples focus on the wedding day and the honeymoon and spend all of their time getting ready for this one short period of time. They forget that the marriage is what will last a lifetime. Song of Songs does not miss this reality. Much of this book deals with the need to build a relationship and maintain a romantic and growing life of intimacy in marriage.

When we come to 5:2, we discover that the wedding and the honeymoon are over. We don't know how much time has passed, but the couple is now into their married life. This is kind of a dream sequence. The wife says, "I slept but my heart was awake" (5:2). The husband comes home from work. He has been out in the fields tending the sheep and is covered with dew. He has something specific on his mind.

As he comes to the door you can almost hear him, "I had to work late, dear. My head is covered with dew, but I'm home now." Then notice all of the pet names he throws in: "my sister, my darling, my dove, my flawless one." Can you guess what he has in mind?

Her response is found in verse 3, "I have taken off my robe—must I put it on again? I have washed my feet—must I soil them again?" In other words, "Do I have to get up and let you in?" This is a Middle Eastern way of saying, "Not tonight, I've got a headache." Even in the Song of Songs marriage is not idealized to the point of being unrealistic. Song of Songs helps us see that romance and sexual expression in the covenant of marriage is a beautiful gift from God; it is to be celebrated. But the realities of life always enter in and make it critical that we work at maintaining a healthy romantic relationship, even when schedules are full and tensions can mount.

8 What are some of the "realities of life" that can dampen the fires of romance for a married couple?

9 What are some of the ways that a couple can stoke the fires of romance and continue to develop intimacy in their marriage?

10 Most of us know a few couples who have a vibrant and joy-filled marriage. Think about a couple you know that fits into this category. What do they do in their marriage that is a great example for other couples?

Closing Reflection

Take a few minutes of silence for personal reflection . . .

Who are some of the healthy and godly couples you know that have a vibrant romantic relationship? What can you learn from these kind of couples?

Take time to respond to this closing question . . .

What are some of the greatest prayer needs for married couples today? Close your small group by praying together . . .

Take time as a group to pray for marriages.

- Pray for healing and restoration in marriages that are strained.
- Pray for those who are widows and widowers. Pray for the comfort and strength of God to fill their hearts.
- Lift up words of thanksgiving for marriages that are strong and healthy.

Old Testament Life Challenge
A Time to Praise

Husbands and wives need to learn to praise the good they see in each other. Maybe you need to discover the dovelike beauty that is in the eyes of your spouse. If you have not looked deeply into your spouse's eyes in a long time, it is time to start gazing again.

A loving husband should find things about his wife that he celebrates and tells her on a regular basis. In turn, his wife should receive these words of celebration. She should not say, "No. It's not true. I'm not that pretty." She needs to receive his words of praise and drink in his love. In the same way, a wife should compliment and affirm the good attributes she sees in her husband. When she sees something in his appearance or character that is praiseworthy, she should let him know. He also needs to learn to receive her words of blessing.

If you are married, commit to actively work at blessing and building up your spouse. Speak words of love, write a note, buy flowers, plan a special date, make an effort to be romantic.

Solomon: Extreme Wisdom

1 KINGS 3:7-28; PROVERBS

Introduction

Have you ever done anything really stupid?

The truth is that we have all done more stupid things than we want to remember. However, when we identify the reality of our poor decisions, we become profoundly aware of our need for God's wisdom. Admitting that we have said things we regret, hurt people we love deeply, let anger rule our responses, followed lust where we should have never gone, and done many other unwise things is the beginning of growing in wisdom.

The book of Proverbs was given by God to help us identify what is wise and what is foolish. It teaches us to do less stupid things and to grow in our ability to live wisely.

Looking at Life

Tell about a time you did something really foolish that you wish you could go back and do differently!

1

If you could go back and do it over again, what would you do differently?

Learning from the Word
Read: 1 Kings 3:7-28

MEETING SOLOMON

At the beginning of 1 Kings, David is dying. This leads to a lot of intrigue and jockeying for the throne. The first few chapters of 1 Kings reveal the chaos that existed in the kingdom, but God is still at work. He promised in 2 Samuel 7 that one of David's sons would be king after him, and that's exactly what happened here.

In chapter 3 God comes to Solomon in a dream. God says to Solomon, "Ask me for whatever you want—anything." This is an interesting test. If God were to offer most people a blank check, they would go after the standard list of riches, power, and all the stuff of the world. Solomon's response is amazing. He prays for wisdom!

2

What do you learn about Solomon's view of God in this passage?

What do you learn about his view of himself?

3

In Solomon's day, as in our day, many people valued wealth, power, and authority more than wisdom. God is clear that wisdom is more valuable than any of these other things. Why does God esteem wisdom above so many of the things we think are so valuable?

Read: Proverbs 1:1-7

WISDOM DEFINED

In the Old Testament, wisdom is fundamentally the ability to make right decisions. In ancient times, wisdom was not primarily about how high your IQ was or how educated you were. It was not primarily about information. In our day, we tend to confuse information with wisdom. Do you ever feel overloaded with information? That's not wisdom. Wisdom was extremely practical. It was the ability to discern what the noble, constructive, and God-honoring course of action would be in actual, real-life situations. Then, wisdom was making the choice to do it. That's wisdom.

A fool, by contrast, was not primarily an ignorant person—not primarily someone with a low IQ. Folly, in the Old Testament, was a problem of the will, not the mind. At its heart, folly is rebellion against God, moral depravity, spiritual blindness, and social irresponsibility toward others. A fool might know all the answers, but he couldn't seem to do the wise thing.

We often think of fools needing wisdom, and they do. According to these opening verses of Proverbs, who needs the wisdom that can be found in this book, and what does Proverbs offer each of us?

4

How does the biblical understanding of wisdom differ from our modern understanding of what makes a person intelligent?

5

> As effective as the Proverbs are as a guide to success, they will always be misleading if used as magical sayings, which would always automatically bring results.
>
> —DAVID HUBBARD

Read: 1 John 1:9; Exodus 20:13; and Proverbs 26:4

UNDERSTAND THE TYPE OF LITERATURE YOU ARE READING
If we are going to benefit from Proverbs, it is crucial that we understand the kind of teaching Proverbs is meant to give us. If we don't get this right, we will get really frustrated along the way. It is important that we clarify the nature of a proverb, as we have other kinds of literature in the Old Testament. A proverb is a specific genre and must be read in light of this.

There are many and varied types of literature in the Old Testament, but here are three specific kinds:

A law: A law is a command that you must always obey.

A promise: A promise is a guarantee that is always true.

A proverb: A proverb is a catchy observation about the way things *generally* are.

Proverbs are designed to give helpful guidance in real-life situations. But they are not absolutes.

6

In light of the definitions given above, identify which of the following passages is a law, a promise, and a proverb:

- 1 John 1:9 is a _____

- Exodus 20:13 is a _____

- Proverbs 26:4 is a _____

What kind of problems might we run into if we try to read a proverb as if it is a law or a promise?

Read: Proverbs 10:19; 19:24; 10:25; 12:1; 30:15; and 19:17

ADOPTING A PROVERB

Proverbs can help shape and transform our lives. The proverbs cover many areas of life, but we are going to look at six specific proverbs and the life transformation they invite us to experience. Each small group member will adopt a proverb. Write your proverb down and put it someplace where you will see it often. Consider memorizing your proverb. Make this statement of wisdom your own and watch how it impacts your life.

A Proverb about Our Words (Proverbs 10:19)

> *When words are many, sin is not absent,*
> *but he who holds his tongue is wise.*

This proverb is pretty straightforward. The more you talk, the more you sin. Thus, one of the simplest ways to cut down on sin is to stop talking so much. A wise person will refrain from speaking in many situations. Sometimes holding our tongue is the best way to show that we are growing in wisdom.

A Proverb about Laziness (Proverbs 19:24)

> *The sluggard buries his hand in the dish;*
> *he will not even bring it back to his mouth!*

This parable is a caricature of a person who is lazy. He puts his hand in the nacho bowl and decides it's not worth the energy it will take to transport the food to his mouth. He thinks, "It's too much work. I'll just leave my hand right there. Maybe the wind will blow one of the nachos my way." The point is that no one is ever nurtured by laziness. Lack of action always leads to loss of life. God wants us to use our energy, strength, and abilities for his glory.

A Proverb about Enduring (Proverbs 10:25)

> *When the storm has swept by, the wicked are gone,*
> *but the righteous stand firm forever.*

This proverb acknowledges the fact that storms do come in life. The question is not if, but when! Yet, at the end of the day, God helps the righteous stand strong. Even in the toughest of times we can rest assured that God will be with his people. For those who are facing times that demand endurance, faith, and a steadfast spirit, this is a great proverb.

A Proverb about Discipline (Proverbs 12:1)

> *Whoever loves discipline loves knowledge,*
> *but he who hates correction is stupid.*

We all need to hear the unvarnished truth from people who love us. A wise person listens and learns from these words of discipline. A fool ignores and resists loving correction. If we are going to become the people God wants us to be, we need to become humble enough to accept and even invite discipline. If we only surround ourselves with people who agree with us and affirm everything we do, we will never grow. Proverbs gives this powerful word of wisdom, "Wounds from a friend can be trusted, but an enemy multiplies kisses" (Proverbs 27:6).

A Proverb about Selfishness (Proverbs 30:15)

> *The leech has two daughters.*
> *"Give! Give!" they cry.*
> *There are three things that are never satisfied,*
> *four that never say, "Enough!"*

Have you ever seen a leech? They are natural-born bloodsuckers. They attach onto a host body with both ends of their little bodies. That's where the idea of "two daughters" comes from. Two daughters both say, "Give! Give!" Because the leech is a taker, it is never expected to give anything back. A leech never hooks onto you and says, "I have a gift I'd like to give to you." Leeches only make withdrawals, never deposits. This proverb is pointing to people who take and take and never learn to give. Clearly they are not walking in the way of wisdom.

A Proverb about Generosity (Proverbs 19:17)

> *He who is kind to the poor lends to the LORD,*
> *and he will reward him for what he has done.*

If you're kind to the poor, it's like lending to God. Maybe the generosity factor in your life needs to be turned up a notch. What better thing can you do with your resources than share with the poor and be generous toward God? Maybe this is the proverb you need to take with you as you ask God to help you develop a generous spirit.

7 After you have read the six proverbs listed above and reflected on the brief commentary on each, take time to pray about which proverb you want to adopt as your own. Tell your group which proverb you adopted and why it struck your heart.

The proverb I will adopt is: _____

8 If you follow the teaching of the proverb you adopted, how might your life change in the coming month?

9 If a person went through life ignoring the wisdom in the proverb you adopted, what consequences might come their way?

In light of what you have learned from the proverb you adopted, how can your small group members pray for you to grow in wisdom? Remember, wisdom is more about a transformed life than it is about raw knowledge.

10

Closing Reflection

Take a few minutes of silence for personal reflection . . .

How does God want you to grow in wisdom? How can the book of Proverbs help you in your quest for greater levels of wisdom?

Take time to respond to these closing questions . . .

How can followers of Christ use the book of Proverbs to help them grow in wisdom? What are practical ways to incorporate the teaching of proverbs into our daily life?

Close your small group by praying together . . .

Use the answers that were shared in response to Question 10 in this study as a springboard into praying for wisdom in the lives of your small group members.

Old Testament Life Challenge

A Time for Silence

Henry Nouwen writes about the value of silence and learning to hold our tongue in a wonderful little book called *The Way of the Heart*. He tells about the early Christian wisdom figures who recommended that followers of Christ engage in the practice of silence. This is valuable for many reasons, but one of the most important is that it is hard to talk without sinning.

Consider taking a vow of silence for an hour or set aside a whole day for silence. If your schedule does not allow you to take a full day, then try going a day where you only say what you must. Let your words be as few as possible. When you practice this discipline of silence, you will discover many amazing things. Here are some of the lessons learned in silence:

- You can live without getting in the last word in every situation.

- You can survive without trying to make sure you control how everybody else thinks about you.
- You don't have to win every argument.
- Other people have great ideas, insights, and can figure things out without your input.
- You can go for days without drawing attention to yourself.

As you learn the wisdom of silence, you might discover that there is a new and better way to live. Of course the goal is not to stop talking. The discipline of silence is a tool to help you listen more, to choose your words more carefully, and to lower the sin level in your life.

Life Application: Battling Laziness

For those who wrestle with passivity, procrastination, inertia, or apathy, Proverbs 19:24 might be a wake-up call. If this proverb strikes a chord for you, then identify one area of life where you are struggling with procrastination. What will it take for you to move into action in this area? Who can keep you accountable? What can you do to battle laziness and begin to take specific steps forward toward transformation in this area of your life?

Solomon: Extreme Folly

NUMBERS 33:51–52; DEUTERONOMY 17:14–20; 33:29; 1 KINGS 3:1–3; 9:1–9;
10:14–29; 11:1–8, 40

Introduction

How does a person go from being the wisest man on the earth to a man
buried neck deep in folly? How does a person move from being sensitive
toward God to living a life of radical disobedience?

The truth is, nobody sets out to experience this kind of fall—least of
all Solomon. If you had asked him early in his life and kingship,
"Solomon, do you think you will stray from the path of wisdom and end
up living like a fool?" he would have been shocked that you even asked.
Yet that is exactly what happened.

Solomon's life is a road map that we might call "the way to disaster"!
His descent from the heights of wisdom to the depths of folly is
heartbreaking. When we study his life, we can identify four distinct
detours he took that led him on this downward spiral. By looking closely
at Solomon's mistakes, we can learn to avoid them and the high price that
always comes with folly.

Looking at Life

What are some of the detours that followers of Christ encounter as they
seek to walk with Jesus and grow in wisdom?

1

Why is it critically important that we learn to identify these detours and
stay on the path of wisdom?

Learning from the Word
Read: 1 Kings 3:1–3; Numbers 33:51–52; Deuteronomy 33:29

DETOUR 1: ALLOWING A LITTLE WIGGLE ROOM

The first step in Solomon's downward spiral was to leave a little wiggle room in his commitment. It all began with areas of compromise that many people may have thought were not that important. Of course, a little wiggle room became a lot of wiggle room in a short time. In 1 Kings 3:3 we read: "Solomon showed his love for the LORD by walking according to the statutes of his father David, *except* that he offered sacrifices and burned incense on the high places."

When we read the word "except," we know Solomon is in trouble. Once we hear this word, we don't even need to know what comes next. This word is a clear indicator that Solomon has decided to leave some wiggle room in his devotion. He will try to love God and be devoted, *except for a few areas.*

Can you imagine a husband coming to his wife and saying, "Honey, I love you and I promise to be faithful to you, except. . . ." What can he say after that that's going to make any difference? The simple fact that he says "except" is a guarantee that he will be in deep water.

2

What are some of the areas Solomon allowed for some wiggle room when it came to obeying God?

How do you think Solomon rationalized these "small" compromises?

3

What are some of the areas Christians today tend to leave a little wiggle room in their obedience to God?

How do we rationalize our "partial" obedience?

What is one area in which you are tempted to leave a little wiggle room? How can your small group members help you walk in greater obedience in this area of your life?

4

Read: Deuteronomy 17:14–20; 1 Kings 10:14–29

DETOUR 2: ASSUMING YOU ARE THE EXCEPTION TO THE RULE
Another step in the downward spiral from wisdom to folly is to assume that you are the exception to the rule. You are above God's rules. At this point in the spiral, you don't dispute the rules. You don't disagree with them. In fact, you agree that they're fine for most people. But you just think that you're a little more mature and a little more sophisticated than others. You can handle it. You don't have to follow God's rules as closely as everybody else does.

The problem with anything less than total obedience is that you're the one who then gets to choose what you will submit to and what "really doesn't matter." When this happens, you become your own king. You become your own god. This becomes a form of idolatry.

In Deuteronomy 17:14–20 God gives some specific rules for how a king of Israel should conduct himself. List these in the spaces provided below. In 1 Kings 10:14–29 we get a report on how Solomon conducted himself as a king. How does his behavior fit with the instructions given in Deuteronomy? Use the space provided below to record Solomon's behavior in each area.

5

Rule for kings of Israel

How Solomon did in
following this rule

-

-

-

-

-

-

-

-

-

-

Why do you think there is such a discrepancy between God's command and Solomon's actions as king?

6

Imagine you have hit a point where you know God's Word is clear about a specific action being sinful, but you have decided it is acceptable in your circumstances. What would you want a Christian friend to say or do to help you resist the temptation to rationalize sin in your life?

Read: 1 Kings 11:1-8

DETOUR 3: FAILING TO DEAL WITH PREDISPOSED WEAKNESSES

The third step in the downward spiral from wisdom to folly is failing to deal with predisposed weaknesses. We all have them. But when we refuse to look at them and resist turning away from them, we are headed for trouble.

Solomon was not particularly discriminating when it came to women. He seemed to love them all! Even when God gave clear commands about this, he kept right on marrying women who were forbidden. We must stop and wonder why he struggled so much in this area of his life.

When we look back through Solomon's personal history, some clues begin to rise to the surface. Solomon had been exposed to sexual struggles through his whole life. If you read through the Old Testament, you discover that David's family had one of the most dysfunctional households around. There is a good chance that Solomon's problems stretched all the way to David's bedroom. The sins and weaknesses of his parents infected his life and impacted him for a lifetime!

How have you seen the sins of one generation impact and infect the next generation (both in the Bible and in your life)?

7

What is one family sin that you have to guard yourself against because you have a family history that gives you a predisposition toward this area of struggle?

8

How can your small group members pray for you and encourage you in your efforts to resist sin in this area of your life? You may want to pause and pray together right now.

Read: 1 Kings 9:1–9; 11:40

DETOUR 4: IGNORING CORRECTION

The final step on this downward spiral is to ignore or to silence corrective words. This is one of the surest signs of disaster. When a person is sliding down into sin and rebellion, and he or she refuses to listen to someone who comes with wise and loving correction, such an individual is in a dangerous place. And when that person has already followed the first three detours, sin has a way of deafening one's ears so they have a difficult time hearing God's voice.

As Solomon grew older, he wandered further and further from God. He did not listen to warnings but did things his own way. God continued to call Solomon to a place of repentance, but he refused to respond. Eventually God used a servant named Jeroboam to threaten the kingdom with division if things did not change. Rather than become humble and repent, Solomon remained hardhearted. We read these shocking words: "Solomon tried to kill Jeroboam, but Jeroboam fled to Egypt, to Shishak the king, and stayed there until Solomon's death" (1 Kings 11:40). Rather than repent and hear God's warning, Solomon ignored correction.

9

When Solomon finished building the temple of the Lord, God appeared to him and told him what would happen if he walked in obedience and the consequences if he chose to live in disobedience. What were the blessings of obedience God placed before Solomon? What were the consequences of disobedience?

Blessings of obedience	Consequences of disobedience
•	•
•	•
•	•
•	•

10

Tell about a time that someone lovingly warned you about a possible danger area in your life and how this helped you.

What may have happened if you had ignored their warning?

Closing Reflection

Take a few minutes of silence for personal reflection . . .

Where might you see yourself heading down the path toward folly? Think through the four detours and identify any which seems current for you.

Take time to respond to this closing question . . .

Which of the four detours discussed in this study would you most likely "fall for"?

Close your small group by praying together . . .

Take time to pray for God to break the downward spiral from wisdom to folly in the lives of your small group members. If Solomon could fall into this pattern, none of us is exempt! Pray for the power of God's Holy Spirit to fill each person as we learn to break the cycle of pride and sin and to grow in humble obedience.

Old Testament Life Challenge
95 Percent Devotion Is 5 Percent Short!

There is no such thing as partial commitment. When you begin with an exception clause, you never arrive at full devotion. Here is a good life lesson for all followers of Christ: 95 percent devotion to God is 5 percent short. God calls us to complete surrender to his leading in our lives. He does not do this to take away our fun or limit our freedom. He calls us to full devotion because he knows we will find fullness of joy and true freedom when we are 100 percent committed to him.

We need to look honestly at our lives and ask some hard questions:

- Where am I allowing wiggle room in my devotion to God?
- How am I being tempted to wander from God because of the areas in which I am allowing wiggle room?
- What are some of the consequences I may face if I keep allowing this wiggle room in my life?
- What is it going to take for me to be 100 percent devoted in this area of my life?

When we leave any wiggle room in our commitment to God, we are leaving the door open for disaster. If we leave it open just a crack, sooner or later the wind will blow it all the way. Solomon got started with a little wiggle room and ended up in radical disobedience. Do all you can in the coming week to remove wiggle room from your life.

Job: Where Is God When It Hurts?

THE BOOK OF JOB

Introduction

Suffering, loss, and pain are part of life. We all experience suffering before our lives come to a close. Some people will face larger doses of suffering than others. Gerald L. Sitzer tells his story of loss in a book entitled *A Grace Disguised*. His wife, mother, and daughter were in a head-on collision when a drunk driver crossed over the road and hit them. Gerald was driving and watched as the lives of three generations of his family died. He poignantly writes of the struggle to make sense of the tragedy with these words:

> *Loss creates a barren present, as if one were sailing on a vast sea of nothingness. Those who suffer loss live suspended between a past for which they long and a future for which they hope. They want to return to the harbor of the familiar past and recover what was lost . . . or they want to sail on and discover a meaningful future that promises to bring them life again. . . . Instead, they find themselves living in a barren present that is empty of meaning.*

These honest words express what many people feel in the midst of the pain and loss of suffering.

Looking at Life

Tell about a time you faced deep pain and suffering in your life.

How did you experience God's presence with you during this time?

Learning from the Word
Read: Job 1:1–10, 20–22; 2:1–10; 3:1–8

JOB'S STORY IS OUR STORY

The problems in the book of Job are the problems of the human race. They're the problems we all face. We can all see ourselves in the story of Job.

In the beginning of this book, everything is as we think it should be. Job is a pious man. He is so cautious about his spiritual life that he even offers sacrifices for his children *just in case* they have done something wrong that he does not know about. He wonders whether God might be offended and wants to take no chances.

God has given him a wonderful life. He is the richest man in the east, the greatest man in his land. The amount of blessing he experiences seems to be directly proportional to the amount of obedience he offers toward God.

What Job does not know is that trouble is coming to the land of Uz. Job is not expecting it, but it is coming like a tsunami. Uz will be a place where very bad things happen to a very good man. Uz will forever be known as a place where suffering comes with no warning and with no explanation.

2

How does Job's response to the suffering he faces change as he walks deeper into this experience?

Is there anything about Job's response that surprises you?

3

Some Christians feel it is wrong to honestly express how they feel during times of pain and struggle. Why do you think some followers of Christ feel this way?

4

What are some of the ways in which we can express our heartache and sorrow in the midst of our suffering?

What might happen if we lock our hurt up in our hearts and refuse to express it to God and others?

Read: Job 2:11–13; 4:7; 8:4; and 11:13–15

SOME THINGS NEVER CHANGE

Philip Yancey notes that the arguments voiced by Job's friends are still repeated in Christian churches today. Suffering people have told him that those who make their suffering worse are often well-meaning Christians who are confused about this very issue. These are some of the lines that well-intentioned but confused Christians might use:

- "The reason that you're in the hospital is spiritual warfare. If you were just standing strong and walking in the power of Jesus, Satan would be defeated. You'd be delivered."
- "God promises to heal if we have enough faith. If you will pray with enough faith, you will be healed." (Implication—if you're not healed, you're not praying with enough faith.)
- "God has handpicked you to suffer to bring him greater glory. You just need to thank him for the pain you're suffering, because it's glorifying him."
- "Your suffering is a wake-up call. It's a punishment for sin. You need to figure out what you've done wrong and repent."

5

Job's friends begin by simply sitting with him in silence. What is the value of simply being with someone who is going through a time of suffering?

Tell about a time someone sat with you at a time of deep need and tell about what their presence meant to you.

6

After seven days of silence, Job's friends begin to speak. Each of them gives a theory on why Job is suffering. What message does each of Job's friends try to convey?

7

What can you learn from the example (both good and bad) of Job's friends? How will this shape the way you walk with others as they are facing times of suffering?

Read: Job 38:1–18; 40:1–14; 42:1–6

GOD SPEAKS

Job gets his wish. He wants God to show up and talk with him. God answers Job out of the storm! What do you think that moment was like? Do you think there was a little drama? Do you think the atmosphere changed when God showed up in a storm? God says, "OK, Job, let's have a face off!" Then, for the next four chapters, God speaks! Job and his friends become quiet. Over and over God asks Job about how the creation came into being. He asks him about specific animals. He puts Job on the witness stand, but Job has little to say!

Part of what's happening is that God is reminding Job that he has a finite mind and a limited point of view. Only God can see the whole story. Ellen Davis, an Old Testament scholar, notices that God's questions actually give great insight into the kind of person he is. He is the kind of God who creates in such a way that the morning stars sing together and the angels shout for joy! In this portion of Job, God's creative beauty shines through and his delight in creation is clear to see.

8

Some people see the book of Job as the story of God on trial. In light of these passages, it becomes clear that Job (representing people) is on trial. Try to put yourself in Job's place at this moment. What do you think he was feeling?

9

What do you learn about the character and nature of God from Job 38–41?

10

In the end, God does not answer Job's questions about why he has faced such incredible suffering. However, God does reveal his own power, presence, and character to Job in the midst of his suffering. Respond to the following statement: In our times of loss and pain, seeing God gives more strength and hope than having answers to all of our questions.

Closing Reflection

Take a few minutes of silence for personal reflection . . .

God uses his people to offer care to each other in times of loss and suffering. How can you make yourself available to be with another person who needs someone sitting at their side?

Take time to respond to these closing questions . . .

What person or family in your church is going through a painful time and could use the care and love of your small group members? What kind of care can you extend as individuals and as a small group?

Close your small group by praying together . . .

Close your small group with a time of prayer for those you know who are living in the land of Uz. Ask God to meet them in a new and powerful way. Pray for strength for them to make it through. Also pray that God will bring friends alongside of them who will sit with them, love them, and see them through.

Old Testament Life Challenge

Mourning Times 2

When we mourn with those who mourn and sit with those who are hurting, we are not trying to fix them. We don't come to give some clever advice that will make everything better. One of the greatest gifts we give is our presence. It is interesting to note that the silence of Job's friends was brilliant. It was a gift. In dramatic contrast, their words became torment.

Do you have friends who will sit with you through a time of suffering? Do you have people who will sit quietly with you just for the sake of offering support? If so, give thanks to God. Also, ask yourself who would be comforted by your presence if they were hurting. Do you have people you can sit with when they are in need of a friend?

If not, commit to make time to deepen your relationships and be sure to make yourself available to those who are in need.

The Divided Kingdom: What Puts Community at Risk

1 KINGS 12:1-17, 25-33; 15:1-3; 2 CHRONICLES 15:8-16:12

Introduction

The time of the divided kingdom is one of the saddest sections in the Old Testament. What began as the magic kingdom under David became the tragic kingdom under David's successors. What started out as Camelot under Solomon, deteriorated into civil war and chaos after Solomon's death. The unity and community that had been experienced for over a hundred years was soon to be shattered.

During this time in history we witness the demise of the community of ancient Israel. Although this was a heart-breaking time in their history, we can learn a great deal from their mistakes and can avoid taking the path that led them to ruin. One of the reasons we study the Old Testament is to learn from the past so that we will not repeat the same mistakes and enter into the same folly. Historians tell us that those who do not remember the past are condemned to repeat it. By God's grace we can discover the factors that contributed to the downfall of the community of ancient Israel and see what puts biblical community at risk. Once these things have been identified, we can avoid these risk factors and build a biblically functioning community that is marked by an enduring spirit of unity.

Looking at Life

As you look at the church in our day and age, what are some of the things that lead to disunity and conflict in the local church?

1

63

Learning from the Word
Read: 1 Kings 12:1-17

RISK FACTOR 1: FAILING TO BE A SERVANT LEADER

Nothing puts community at risk more than a leader who takes advantage of people for selfish gain. Those who never learn the principle of being a servant leader will watch the erosion of community all around them. By contrast, when a leader uses his or her position and power to serve others, this generates loyalty and strengthens community.

At a church in Grand Rapids, Michigan, the staff members talk about having an A-WICS attitude. This came from one staff member who was often heard saying, "Any way I can serve!" Over and over opportunities to serve presented themselves and she kept saying, "Any way I can serve." Even when a task or project was not in her area of ministry or under her job description, she kept looking for ways to serve and support others.

At some point along the way, the pastor coined the phrase, "An A-WICS Attitude." This term describes a person who is ready to say:

Any Way I Can Serve!

2

Rehoboam received two very different kinds of counsel about how he should rule Israel. What were the two conflicting recommendations, and why do you think Rehoboam chose the advice that he did?

3

Finish *one* of the following statements:

- I once served under a leader (in the church, at work . . .) who had the heart of a servant. This leader impacted me and others in the following ways . . .
- I once served under a leader who had a hard time serving others but STILL expected them to be in the role of serving. I will always remember this leader because . . .

Who are some of the people in your life whom God calls you to serve, and what are some steps you can take to grow as a servant?

4

What makes it hard to serve these people?

Read: 1 Kings 12:25–33

RISK FACTOR 2: USING SPIRITUAL LANGUAGE FOR SELFISH MOTIVES
Community is at risk when people seek to manipulate others by using spiritual language to accomplish selfish purposes. This happened in the days of the kings, and it still happens today. Every time someone seeks to leverage another person with hyperspiritual language, we must be cautious and make sure we know their motives.

Jeroboam manipulated people using religious language for his personal, political agenda. It is clear that he was not concerned about the people truly worshiping God. He just wanted to be sure their hearts did not turn back to Jerusalem and the king who ruled there. This still happens in churches today. When people use God-talk in dogmatic terms and in demanding tones so that they can get what they want, that's spiritual manipulation. Every time someone uses spiritual language to advance his or her personal agenda, it is a recipe for broken community. We must learn to have our antennas up so that we can identify when this is happening.

What are some of the ways people today try to use spiritual language to leverage others to do what they want?

5

Share about a time when someone tried to manipulate you with superspiritual language.

6 How can we identify when we are being manipulated in this way?

What can we do to resist when others are trying to leverage us with spiritual language?

Read: 1 Kings 15:1–3

RISK FACTOR 3: FOLLOWING GOD HALFHEARTEDLY

God calls us to be fully devoted followers. He wants 100 percent from us. When we follow him with a halfhearted devotion, we will see community erode all around us. This is a huge risk factor.

There are really two kinds of Christians when it comes to the matter of devotion. First are those Christians who are fully devoted followers of Christ. These are people who live with a deep level of surrender and commitment before God. When God leads, they follow. They understand that their entire lives are under the lordship of Jesus Christ, not just a few selected areas they want to devote.

Second, there are Christians who are half-devoted. They give God some of their heart, some obedience, and some devotion. They want God, but they also want to cling to the things of the world. These people are half full of God, but they are also filled with all kinds of things that poison their hearts and destroy the community God longs to build.

7 What are some indicators that we are growing toward being fully devoted followers of Christ?

What are some of the signs that we are becoming halfhearted in our devotion?

What is one step you believe God wants you to take in your effort to be fully devoted to his purposes for your life?

8

Read: 2 Chronicles 15:8–16:12

RISK FACTOR 4: TURNING AWAY FROM GOD
A fourth factor that puts community at risk is when we turn our hearts away from God. Sometimes a follower of God does not understand something that happens in his or her life and then lets his or her heart become cold toward God. Every time we turn from God, we open the door for conflict and division in community.

Abraham Lincoln is a dramatic contrast to Asa, the king of Judah. Lincoln was president in the United States of America during a time of national crisis. The nation was divided. More Americans died during the civil war than all Americans in all the other wars. It was a time that would test the faith of any leader. But during that time, Lincoln relied on God, and he also led the nation to rely on God. He wrote, "I have been driven, many times, to my knees by the overwhelming conviction that I had nowhere else to go."

How do you see Asa's relationship with God, and his faith, change during this account of his life?

9

Τhe cross is laid on every Christian. The first Christ-suffering which every man must experience is the call to abandon the attachments of this world. . . . We surrender ourselves to Christ in union with His death—we give over our lives to death. . . . When Christ calls a man, He bids him come and die.

—DIETRICH BONHOEFFER

10 Tell about Christians you have known who finished strong as they came to the end of their lives. What action or attitude did they model that you would love to adopt into your own life?

Closing Reflection

Take a few minutes of silence for personal reflection . . .

Which of these four risk factors do you tend to fall into most easily, and why does this happen?

Take time to respond to this closing question . . .

What is one current relationship in your life that your small group could pray and so develop a stronger expression of community?

Close your small group by praying together . . .

One of the most amazing verses in all the Bible is found in 2 Chronicles 16:9: "For the eyes of the LORD range throughout the earth to strengthen those whose hearts are fully committed to him." God is searching all across the world looking into the hearts of each one of us. What does he see? A heart full of God or a heart half full? He strengthens those whose hearts are fully devoted, fully committed to him.

Take time to pray for your small group members to surrender their lives fully to God. Allow time for the Holy Spirit to uncover areas where people have become halfhearted and pray for a new level of devotion and submission.

With malice toward none; with charity for all; with firmness in the right, as God gives us to see the right, let us strive on to finish the work we are in; to bind up the nation's wounds; to care for him who shall have borne the battle, and for his widow, and his orphan—to do all which may achieve and cherish a just and lasting peace, among ourselves, and with all nations.

—ABRAHAM LINCOLN

Old Testament Life Challenge
Guarding Our Path

Each of us needs to carefully examine our attitudes and actions. Do we build community or tear it down? Are we living lives that strengthen the congregation we are part of or tear it apart?

If something has gotten between you and God, it is time to deal with it. If you are no longer trusting in him, it is time for a change. If you have turned away from him, it is time to turn back. Boldly declare, "I will not end up like Asa. I want to be strong to the end!"

It may be helpful to reflect on the words of Proverbs 3:5–8:

> *Trust in the Lord with all your heart*
> *and lean not on your own understanding;*
> *in all your ways acknowledge him,*
> *and he will make your paths straight.*
> *Do not be wise in your own eyes;*
> *fear the Lord and shun evil.*
> *This will bring health to your body*
> *and nourishment to your bones.*

In those places where you may trust in yourself and not in God, ask God for forgiveness. Then ask him to give you strength to trust him, not yourself.

LEADER'S NOTES

CONTENTS

David: Developing a Heart for God

THE HEART
of a Leader

The heart of this message is the condition of the hearts of God's people. God is deeply concerned about our hearts. He wants the throne of our heart to be his dwelling place. The problem is, there are so many other things that are battling for the place of supremacy in our lives.

In this message we look at the life of King David and discover that he had the same struggles we face. He loved God with all his heart, but he faced constant temptations to let other things push God off the throne. As we look at David's lifelong desire to yield his heart fully to God, we will discover that we too can develop a heart that beats passionately for God. We can also learn to place God first in our lives and avoid letting other things rule in our hearts.

THE PRAYER
of a Leader

Like David, every follower of Christ will face the lifelong challenge to keep God firmly on the throne of his or her heart. Your preparation and communication of this message in your small group will be a journey of self-examination.

For you to communicate God's message with clarity and integrity, you will need to invite the Holy Spirit to search your own heart. Is God fully enthroned in your life? Does he rule in your heart? Are there people, habits, life patterns, fears, or anything else that have begun to take a place of supremacy? Come before God with deep humility and ask him to reveal any idol, any alternative to God, that may be alive in your heart. You may want to meditate on Psalm 51 as you prepare to lead this small group.

Question 1

There is more written about David (and by David), than any other character in the Old Testament. Hundreds and hundreds of books have been written about his life. In this Old Testament Challenge study, we will focus primarily on the years of David's kingship.

Many people are familiar with the story of David. They may have grown up seeing his life as a shepherd boy, his battle with Goliath, and his

LEADER'S NOTES

ascension to the throne played out on the two-dimensional world of a flannelgraph in Sunday school classes. Prior to 2 Samuel David was a shepherd tending his father's flocks around Bethlehem. Samuel, the prophet of Israel, is led to the home of Jesse and is called by God to anoint David as the new king.

Soon David fights the giant, Goliath. He defeats Goliath and becomes famous in the land. Over time, King Saul becomes incredibly jealous of David and threatens his life so much that David has to flee. He then finds himself in the desert, wandering for years, separated from his family and the kingdom. In 2 Samuel 5, David finally steps into the role of Israel's king. He conquers Jerusalem, defeats the Philistine army, and begins his kingship. It may seem as if this would be the beginning of David's glory days. But his time in the desert, before he ascended to the throne, was actually some of the most formative years of David's life.

Questions 2–4

The king of Israel was dancing with all his might—in his underwear. David worshiped the Lord with complete abandon and disregard for what anyone else might think. This included his wife Michal, who was the daughter of Saul. Michal was disgusted and offended to see her husband, the king, dancing around the kingdom in his ephod. She was sure this would not be good for public relations. It was certainly going to make the next morning's paper. She was incredibly distressed. But David didn't care, for he was worshiping God with all his might. His attention was fixed and focused and lost in the glory of God.

Imagine what it might look like to be free in your worship of God. What impact would it have on you as a worshiper if you had no concern for what the person next to you sounded like or what you sounded like to them? What if you did not worry about what other people might think of you if you were truly free in worship? How would it feel to be so lost in the glory and wonder of God that you stopped thinking about what others were doing or thinking?

In 2 Samuel 6:22 David tells his wife Michal, "I will become even more undignified than this, and I will be humiliated in my own eyes." It is as if David is telling his wife, "You think this is bad? Just wait until I get going. Wait until I start worshiping God with all my might."

The truth is that many people have grown up in a church where worship of God was seen as a very "dignified" thing. Everyone stood properly with their nice clip-on ties or neatly pressed dresses. They sang from their hymnals, knew when to stand and sit, and followed a clearly printed order of worship. It was a proper thing.

This is not the picture we have of King David. He was passionate, reckless, invested, and even undignified. David's example can become God's invitation for us to enter a deeper, richer, messier kind of worship.

Questions 5–7

Temptation comes to David, and he falls for it—hook, line, and sinker! Not only does David fall into this sin, but he spirals downward deeper into deception by trying to cover his tracks. His sin of adultery, followed by murder, and the subsequent actions end up costing David more than he ever dreamed.

When you face temptation, as we all do, who is on the throne? Do you yield to the enticement or does God's power fill you and allow you to resist? Are you giving in to the same sin over and over? Are you expending large amounts of energy covering your tracks and trying to hide your sin?

When you look at the temptations you face right now, who is on the throne of your life? What causes you to lust and want what is not yours? It is important that we look at the story of David and learn from his experience. He was not satisfied by his sin. It did not end with the one act. David's surrender to temptation began a landslide of sin, deceit, and pain. What a powerful reminder for us to resist the enticement of sin and cling to God's plan for our lives.

The New Testament speaks often about temptation and God's power for us to resist the enticements of the devil. Here are a few passages that speak to this topic:

> No temptation has seized you except what is common to man. And God is faithful; he will not let you be tempted beyond what you can bear. But when you are tempted, he will also provide a way out so that you can stand up under it. (1 Corinthians 10:13)

> Submit yourselves, then, to God. Resist the devil, and he will flee from you. (James 4:7)

> For we do not have a high priest who is unable to sympathize with our weaknesses, but we have one who has been tempted in every way, just as we are—yet was without sin. (Hebrews 4:15)

As followers of Christ, God offers the power and strength we need to resist temptations. As we look to him, we can say no to sin and yes to God.

Questions 8–10

God is outraged by David's sin. Sometimes we can rationalize our sin and convince ourselves that it is not a big deal. God, however, never looks the other way. He sees David's sin and is ready to deal with it. God sends Nathan to confront the wayward king. Nathan tells David a story about a selfish wealthy man. When David hears how this rich man took a neighbor's pet lamb and slaughtered it to serve a visitor instead of taking a lamb from his vast flock, the king is fuming mad! In a shocking twist, Nathan looks at David and says, "You are the man."

Most of us like to be a Nathan more than we like to hear from a Nathan. We don't mind speaking for God when someone is not living right. We may even have radar that picks up sin in others with great accuracy. If this is the case, we need to beware. The ministry of Nathan should be extended with a humble heart and often with tears. We should never take joy in bearing bad news. If God calls us to speak to another follower of Christ about their sin, we should do this in love and with deep humility.

We also need to be ready to receive the ministry of Nathan in our lives. When God sends another believer into our lives to raise an issue or uncover a sin, we must be ready to receive this ministry. They have taken a risk by raising an issue in us. We must be willing to hear their words and then seek God to see if this is his word for us. If it is, repentance is in order.

When Nathan confronted David, he could have resisted and run. He did not have to confess and repent, but he did. In response to the conviction God brought into David's heart, he wrote Psalm 51. This psalm captures the heart of confession as well as any passage in the entire Bible. In this prayer we hear David admit his sin, face his own weakness, ask for God's forgiveness, and even begin to express hope for how God might still use him to be a blessing to others in the future. Confession gave birth to forgiveness, and forgiveness brought hope alive. Like David, we need to learn that confession is often the beginning of a healed and restored relationship with God.

The Heights and Depths of Prayer

THE HEART
of a Leader

For over 2,500 years the book of Psalms has been the prayer book of God's people. There is no greater collection of prayers in the history of humanity. The psalms were the prayer book of Jesus. They have guided the prayers of his followers since the church was formed. The church today needs to continue our rich tradition of letting the psalms form and guide our prayer life.

There are many kinds of psalms, and we will survey these over the coming two sessions. In this session we will focus specifically on the heights and depths of prayer. The psalms lead us to the heights of celebration, praise, and worship, but they also lead us to prayers of honest lament. As a small group leader, take time to evaluate your own prayer life. Do you feel comfortable lifting up both prayers of praise, from the heights of joy, and prayers of lament, from the depths of your sorrow?

THE PRAYER
of a Leader

In this session we ask God to help us make the psalms our prayer book. We will seek to express joy-filled praise as well as the sorrowful depths of lament. To lead a group (large or small) through this process will only happen if you, as the leader, are ready to express your heart to God on both levels.

Take time to prepare your heart by meditating on some of the psalms of praise (99, 103, and 104) and the psalms of lament (22, 42, and 69). Ask God to free you to express the heights of praise and depths of sorrow to him in prayer as you prepare to lead this small group session.

Question 1

The book of Psalms is not just a happy little devotional book filled with uplifting thoughts and inspiring words. It is not given so we can read one page quickly every morning to help us start the day with a positive attitude. Many people turn to Psalms hoping to have this kind of experience. They want every psalm to be a piece of uplifting, inspirational, and devotional literature. About half the time they get what they are looking for. The other half of the time, however, they just may end up disappointed or even confused. If you are looking for a daily devotion that is guaranteed to make you smile, Psalms just might throw you a curve ball!

Why are the psalms so broad in their perspective? Why do these prayers embrace so much joy and yet so much pain? Because this is how we experience life. Each day can bring moments of incredible satisfaction, joy, passion, and fulfillment. Then, right next to these moments we can feel inexpressible heartache and sorrow.

We can wake up one morning feeling happy and peaceful. We are sure it is going to be a wonderful day. By the end of the day, however, something has happened, and our heart is broken. We feel sorrow and must face the reality of the pain in this life.

There are other days we feel down. We are sure there is no reason to get out of bed. But by the end of the day God has surprised us with joy. God has shown up in some way and amazed us with his goodness and his grace. The psalms help us express our prayers to God no matter what the day brings.

Questions 2–5

If you have ever stood at the edge of Niagara Falls or seen the Grand Tetons, you understand how natural praise can be. Nobody has to tell you to say, "Ohhh!" and "Ahhhh!" It just comes out. If you have ever watched a professional or Olympic athlete break a record or make a game-winning shot, no one had to tell you to cheer or clap, it just happens. We burst into celebration and praise when we see, hear, or even taste something that is praiseworthy.

If we can't express our wonder and affirmation, we feel cheated. It leaves us feeling empty. There is something God has placed within us that makes us erupt in praise.

When a human being encounters God, praise must be expressed. When we see that God is all-wise, infinitely powerful, eternal, utterly holy, all-loving, completely merciful, inexhaustibly patient, ceaselessly creative, beautiful, and joy-filled, adoration erupts. It is the natural response. Our experience with God will never be complete until we express the praise, wonder, and adoration that is in our hearts. It can't be some general expression to whoever is listening; it must be lifted to God directly.

When we express our love to God and know he receives and delights in our praise, nothing compares. It just doesn't get any better. That is when we know we're in a relationship with him of reciprocal joy, giving and receiving honor and delight. That is why praise is so important in the life of a follower of Christ.

Psalms of praise have two basic parts. The first part—and it is in most of the praise psalms—is the call to worship. This is the invitation for God's people to enter into his presence and to express their praise to him. Psalm 103 begins:

> Praise the LORD, O my soul;
>> all my inmost being, praise his holy name.
> Praise the LORD, O my soul,
>> and forget not all his benefits—

In a sense the psalmist is calling himself to worship. Before he invites anyone else to worship, he invites himself. Listen to those words, "Praise the LORD, O *my* soul." At the end of Psalm 103 he calls others to worship:

> Praise the LORD, you his angels,
>> you mighty ones who do his bidding,
>> who obey his word.
> Praise the LORD, all his heavenly hosts,
>> you his servants who do his will.
> Praise the LORD, all his works
>> everywhere in his dominion. (Psalm 103:20–22)

David throws open the doors and starts inviting angels, the heavenly host, and everyone and everything in creation to come praise the Lord. At the very end of the psalm he comes back to himself with one final invitation to his own soul. The call to worship is a critical and important part of worship.

Questions 6–10

As we read Psalm 42 we begin to understand the heartbeat of a lament. We can feel the pain! We can hear the despair! Honest complaint comes pouring through. The psalmist holds nothing back. Here are some of the things he expresses with bold honesty:

- My only food, day and night, is my tears.
- Other people are taunting me because it seems God will not deliver.
- I used to gather with God's people for worship, now I can't. My joy and thanksgiving are gone.
- My soul is downcast and disturbed.
- I feel forgotten by God.
- I am oppressed by my enemies.

LEADER'S NOTES

These are not the statements of someone at the top of his spiritual game. This is a far cry from the celebration of Psalm 103. This is a person who feels broken and abandoned. Yet this kind of prayer is acceptable and pleasing to God. When was the last time you dared pray with this kind of bold honesty?

The laments can help us when we face any kind of pain or time of struggle. There are four primary topics that are addressed in the laments.

The fear of enemies. In the laments we hear people crying out to God because they are being attacked by an enemy. Enemies can take many shapes and forms. An enemy could be your boss, a neighbor, a coworker, or everybody on the freeway. It could even be somebody you usually love but are facing conflict with at this time. It could be somebody you're sitting near in church, even the person next to you. Your enemy could be depression, loneliness, fear, or sin. It's whatever or whomever you need deliverance from. God invites you to come to him and cry out for strength to resist the attack you are under today.

The battle with illness. A second category in the laments is the problem of sickness. This can be a physical problem or even the stress you feel because of the burdens of life. Anything that creates stress and pain in your body is included in this kind of lament. In the Hebrew mind-set, emotional and physical pain were both real.

Here's the truth about us: we carry things in our bodies all day. We can be anxious about a test in school, fearful about a work review coming up, or tense about a relationship that is broken. These things can impact our body. Maybe we are facing financial pressures or are worried about a child who is making poor choices. We may be walking around with a churning stomach, stiff necks, aching heads, sweaty palms, and boiling blood. We all know exactly what the psalmist means when he says, "My bones suffer."

The reality of death. The sense of pressure or trouble is often so severe in the psalms of lament that the psalmist speaks of being at the point of death. When he talks about Sheol (NIV translates this word as "grave"), one idea behind this term is that they don't see any way out. Death becomes a picture of a life that feels hopeless and a soul that is in mortal agony.

Of course, there are also times when a lament is about more than fear of death or a sense of utter hopelessness. There were times when the psalmist was under attack and genuinely fearful for his life. Sometimes a prayer of lament will be lifted up by a person who is on the edge of death as a result of an illness or even old age. The reality of death can bring us to a place of honest prayer.

The anxiety of being trapped. The fourth and final specific category in the laments is the anxiety of being trapped. Through the psalms of lament we find images like drowning or being stuck in a pit. The idea is that we all know how it feels to be stuck in a situation we can't seem to get out of. In a prayer of lament we may cry out to God and say, "I'm stuck in a financial pit and I can't get out." We may call out to God because we feel trapped in a painful marriage, habitual sin, destructive relational patterns, or some kind of addiction. In a lament we call to God, admit that we are stuck, and ask him to help get us out of our situation.

LEADER'S NOTES

LEADER'S NOTES

THE HEART
of a Leader

In this small group session we will look at four different kinds of psalms. Each of these categories of psalms helps us speak our heart to God in new and powerful ways. In this session we will actually practice making the psalms our prayer to God. God longs for us to learn to pray in deeper and richer ways, and one of the best tools we have for developing our prayer life is the book of Psalms.

As we learn from the psalms and as they become part of our hearts, we will grow as people of prayer. The psalms will enable us to give voice to our thanks, sorrow, anger, fear, praise, and so much more. The psalms have been an indispensable tool in the spiritual lives and growth of God's people for thousands of years. We need to let them become ours.

THE PRAYER
of a Leader

Each kind of psalm holds the key to unlock a part of our heart and express it to God. From the heights of thanksgiving to the deep sorrow of confession, the psalms help us speak our hearts to God. From the depths of shame because of rebellion against God to the heights of the throne room of God, the psalms will instruct us if we let them. As a leader, take time to let the psalms speak to your heart and prepare you to speak to God. Meditate on the following psalms as you prepare to lead this small group study (Psalms 30, 51, and 119).

Question 1

This is not meant to be a time to critique the ways children learn to pray. Many of the simple childlike prayers have a wonderful way of helping young people begin a life of prayer. The key is that we move beyond memorization to intimate communication.

Questions 2-4

Psalms of thanksgiving explode with celebration for what God has done. Psalms of thanksgiving shift our attention to the mighty acts of God and all he does for his children. God has been good, beyond description. The thanksgiving psalms release the deep gratitude that has been locked up in our hearts. They remind us that God is worthy of being thanked for all of his mighty deeds.

There is a basic structure or movement in the psalms of thanksgiving. They follow this basic format:

1. An admission of need. The psalmist declares an awareness that he was in a time of need. This need could be something specific or general.

2. A cry to God. Next, the psalmist declares that he cried out to God in his time of need. He made his need known and trusted in God to protect, provide, deliver, or meet his need in some other way.

3. An expression of thanks for God's work. Finally, the psalmist identifies the way that God heard his prayer and acted. Then, a natural and joy-filled expression of thanksgiving follows. This prayer of thanks is always rooted in what God has done and how his mighty power has been revealed.

Questions 5–6

Another category of psalms is called penitential psalms. They help us to learn how to do self-examination and to express confession to God. They are open and honest prayers, where we say, "Lord, in the light of your goodness, in the light of your glory, I see myself as I really am and I am sorry. I have sinned. I have wronged you. I have broken your heart." These psalms give voice to our sorrow over sin and also move us to a place of repentance and transformed lives.

We cannot go to a doctor to get X rays that reveal the condition of our heart and soul. Instead, God has given us the penitential psalms to help in this process. It is as if the psalmist is saying, "How can I find out about something that's toxic to my body, that could destroy my soul, paralyze my heart, sear my conscience, and separate me from God, yet I cannot see it? How do I examine my heart?

Each time we read these psalms and make them our own, God helps us see where we need to confess and repent. Sometimes we see the sickness growing in our soul. At other times, we are blind to it. But, always, God is ready to reveal it, if we ask, and to help us deal with our sin.

Once we learn to pray with these psalms of confession, we can naturally begin praying as the Holy Spirit leads us. David's prayer in Psalm 51 is not meant to be simply repeated over and over. It is an example for us to learn from. When we see David's heart and hear his cry, we begin to be authentic in our prayers of confession over our sins!

LEADER'S NOTES

Questions 7-8

There are many ways the psalms were structured by the authors. Psalm 119 is a praise of God's wisdom from beginning to end. The entire psalm, all twenty-two stanzas, is based on the Hebrew alphabet. The first section of eight verses each begins with the first letter of the Hebrew alphabet, Aleph. The final section of eight verses each begins with the last letter, Taw. This is the author's way of saying that the law of God, his wisdom, is all we need for life; it is all inclusive!

This psalm puts life into perspective. God's wisdom is more valuable than anything else in the entire world. We don't often see it this way, but it is true. The Hebrews prized the wisdom of God more than any other possession. God's wisdom warns us and keeps us from stumbling. It is the source of truth and blessing.

God longs for us to come to a place where we love his Word and hunger for it. Reading the Word of God and growing in his wisdom is not a chore but a privilege. It is not a burden we bear but a source of amazing strength in the life of a follower of Christ.

Questions 9-10

Enthronement psalms turn our eyes and hearts to the very throne of God. These are psalms that recognize that this world may have troubles and that earthly leaders might not always be fair, but God is still on the throne. These prayers turn our eyes upward, toward the very dwelling place of God, and remind us that no matter what we face, God is still in charge.

When we turn our eyes off of God, we tend to fixate on ourselves. Every time this happens, peace is stripped away and anxiety sets in. Trust erodes and fear moves into our hearts. We forget that the God who is on the throne is still the Alpha and the Omega, the Beginning and the End, the First and the Last.

When we lift up enthronement prayers, we see God high and lifted up, and life makes sense again.

THE HEART
of a Leader

Get ready to blush! Teaching from Song of Songs is a roller coaster ride of passion, excitement, and intimacy. There is no way to teach this book with integrity and avoid the presence of honest expressions of romantic love and clear longings for sexual fulfillment. If you feel uncomfortable addressing these topics, it is time to pray for God's strength and leading. God celebrates the goodness of human romance, and so should we. If you are married but your relationship is not healthy and filled with romance, let this be a time to seek the Lord for a new flame to begin burning in your marriage.

THE PRAYER
of a Leader

Pray for a new vision of God's love for romance and intimacy. Ask God to help you see marriage and human sexuality the way he does. Pray for your small group members. Some of those in your small group might be in marriages that are just terrific. Others feel trapped in marriages that may be painful. There are also people who are married, but their spouse is not a believer. Almost every possible marital situation is represented in most churches. Take time to pray for each person at their point of need.

Question 1

There are a number of reasons people feel God is against sexual expression. One reason is that this good gift of God has been misused so much that it can appear hurtful or out of control. However, when romance and sexual expression are enjoyed within the bounds of the marriage covenant, God celebrates them. Others have had bad personal experiences and see human sexuality through the lenses of their own pain. Still others have been taught that God is opposed to sex. Sadly, those who should have modeled a healthy physical relationship (their parents) taught them that sexuality is something that is bad, dirty, or evil.

In this small group study we will see that romance and sexual expression within the covenant marriage relationship are a gift and a blessing. They are to be embraced and celebrated.

LEADER'S NOTES

Questions 2–4

WOMEN IN THE ANCIENT WORLD

Notice that the woman is the first to speak in the Song of Songs. She is honest, bold, and clear in what she is longing to have—kisses! We often think of women in the Middle East (especially the ancient Middle East) as being modest and even prudish. We think about the veils and long robes, and we can forget that they were women with the same desires and longings women have today. As we walk through this song, it becomes clear that the woman has a level of desire and passion every bit as powerful as the man has. It also becomes apparent that God is so pleased with her desires (and the man's longing) that he includes all of it in Scripture.

In 1:3 the woman says, "Your name is like perfume." She's captivated by his name. This often happens with deep attraction. We can become fascinated by the name of a person we love. But there is more happening here than just a mere fascination with a name.

A name in the Scriptures generally refers to someone's *identity*, *reputation,* or *character*. This is why the people of God were always careful to honor God's name and never misuse it. God's name was equivalent to his character. Thus, when the woman is saying that her lover's name is like a pleasing fragrance, she is speaking of who he is as a person. She is deeply drawn to the character of this man. He is a man of deep integrity, honesty, and loyalty; he can be trusted.

In 4:1–5 we hear the man praising the woman's beauty. This is the kind of imagery that tends to bog some people down when they read through the Song of Songs. Here are some quick insights that might help make sense of the imagery in this passage.

Her eyes are doves. Doves in that culture were prized, especially for their color. In the sun, they were kind of a translucent gray. This is the man's way of saying he sees her eyes, and they are beautiful.

When you look into somebody's eyes, it's an intimate thing. It's a soul gaze. Their eyes will tell you if they're happy, if they're dancing, if they're sad, if they're beaten down by life. If you are deeply attached to someone, you know the color of their eyes because you have looked in them many times. This man has looked deeply into this pair of eyes.

Her hair is like a flock of goats. This is not a common compliment in our day, but in that culture it made sense. When a large herd of goats came down a hill, they would wind around it in a way that looked quite striking and attractive from a distance. This was his way of saying, "Your hair is thick and wavy. I like how it curls. I just like how it looks."

Questions 5–7

Praying faithfully for married couples is a great gift. God also invites us to cheer and affirm when a marriage is strong and heading in the right direction. We can encourage our married friends, listen to them, and respond in ways that build hope. If a marriage is in trouble, we can encourage our friends to talk with a pastor or see a good Christian counselor. When a marriage is doing well, we can make specific observations about the good parts of the relationship we see and rejoice with our friends. Every marriage needs a cheering section, and it is an honor when we can be part of a chorus of voices that celebrate a good marriage.

Questions 8–10

Even in the strongest most passionate marriages there will be tough times. Every couple needs to be ready for this. If you get married expecting perfect harmony, endless romance, and no conflict, you will be disappointed. The issue is not whether we will face difficult days, it is how we will respond when these times come. These are the days when we need to receive God's power and grace when ours are in short supply. These are the times we need our chorus of friends to support and encourage us. These are the moments that we might need to seek the help of a professional Christian counselor to help us get perspective and tools that will help us move forward and build a marriage that honors God and brings blessing to our hearts.

As Song of Songs continues, there are many expressions of joy, celebrations of beauty, and expressions of commitment to make this relationship last. Song of Songs 8:6–7 is one of the most beautiful sections of the entire book. It is a closing declaration that their love will be unquenchable. In a world where intimacy, romance, and relationships seem to get snuffed out by busyness, apathy, unresolved conflict, financial stresses, poor communication, and selfishness, we need to hear these words. Love seems to get quenched each day, but it does not have to. If you are married, let this be the moment you say that your love will not be quenched. Commit to sitting with your spouse and talking about how you can fan the flames of your marriage. What will it take to rekindle the spark of romance? What habits need to start? What needs to end? Who will keep you accountable to build a healthy relationship? How will you celebrate when you take steps forward on this journey?

Solomon: Extreme Wisdom

THE HEART
of a Leader

The Proverbs were most likely collected as a part of an effort to train and develop a whole new generation of leaders who would serve under Solomon. The purpose of this book was to impart wisdom to all who were willing to receive it. As a leader, open your heart to what God wants to teach you through this session.

Wisdom is the ability to make right decisions that honor God and move us toward his purposes for life. In this small group session all the participants will be challenged to find a proverb that they can carry in their hearts in a way that will transform their lives. This message is about growing to understand and love God's wisdom so much that we long to see it grow in our lives. As a leader, set the tone by coming with a receptive and humble heart.

THE PRAYER
of a Leader

As you prepare to lead this small group, be sure to adopt a proverb from the six key verses in this message (they follow Question 7 in the study). Once you have chosen your proverb, commit it to memory. Spend a week meditating on this verse and let God's wisdom sink deeply into your heart. Ask God to shape your thoughts and actions around its message. Pray for the Holy Spirit to transform your life to reflect this proverb.

Question 1

The opening questions in this study can lead to a light and humorous discussion. They can also lead to a serious and sober discussion. As a leader, don't try to direct where this goes. Let your small group members express their hearts honestly. These responses will help set the direction for your study. Both light and serious responses are appropriate, so welcome both.

Questions 2–3

What was Solomon's greatest legacy and contribution to the people of God? Certainly he brought a time of unparalleled fame and prosperity. His building of the temple ranks near the top of the list. He expanded the borders of Israel. All of these things are noteworthy. But they are not his greatest legacy.

The proverbs are Solomon's greatest contribution to God's people. All through his life he reminded the people that wisdom is a path they must walk every day. More important than Solomon's building projects, expansion of the kingdom, or the time of peace he ushered in is the book of Proverbs and the wisdom that continues to speak to each new generation.

Right after Solomon's prayer in 1 Kings 3 we read a famous story that shows how his wisdom is put to the test in a dramatic way. Two prostitutes come before Solomon. One of their sons has died in the night. Both claim that the living boy is theirs.

"Bring me a sword," Solomon says. "We'll just cut the remaining baby in half and you can each have a portion." In the midst of this judgment the real mother quickly reveals herself. Rather than have her son killed, she is willing to give him up. Of course, Solomon identifies this woman as the true mother and returns her son to her arms.

What a powerful picture of wisdom in action!

Questions 4–5

The first seven verses of Proverbs hold the key to whom this book was written for and why it was written. Proverbs is an urgently important book for followers of Christ today. It is not just a casual collection of affirmations that we can take or leave as we see fit. It was written and given to us to save us from folly, which leads to death. The stakes are high when it comes to this book. If we read it, understand it, and live it out, we are on the path to life. If we ignore Proverbs, we do so at our own peril!

The proverbs themselves warn us to be careful with how we handle and use specific proverbs. Proverbs 26:9 says, "Like a thornbush in a drunkard's hand is a proverb in the mouth of a fool." Just think about what happens when an inebriated, unsteady person grabs a plant full of thorns. They're going to get hurt. The same thing happens when a fool starts using a proverb. He is going to get hurt. She is going to misuse it. And others might get hurt as well.

LEADER'S NOTES

The book of Proverbs invites us to take care and use discernment. The Israelites devoted themselves to this, and so should we. They studied, meditated on, practiced, and committed the proverbs to memory. They celebrated these proverbs, because they found that they changed their lives.

Questions 6

- John 1:9 is a promise.
- Exodus 20:13 is a law.
- Proverbs 26:4 is a proverb.

If we treat a proverb as a law or promise, we will find ourselves frustrated. Laws and promises are always true. But proverbs are true in a general sense. If we try to interpret proverbs as absolutes, we will form theology that is not consistent with what God is seeking to teach us.

Here is one classic example. Some people try to treat Proverbs 22:6 as a law: "Train a child in the way he should go, and when he is old he will not turn from it." This proverb was never intended to be taken as an ironclad guarantee, but many people read it this way. This proverb does not guarantee that if you raise a little girl in the church, teach her the Bible, and do your best, you can be assured that she will become a devoted follower of Jesus. Nor does it mean that if your children go down a destructive or rebellious path, you did a bad job and didn't train them right. Adam and Eve went down the wrong path, but that doesn't mean God (their heavenly Father) did something wrong.

Proverbs 22:6 is simply wisdom for parents. Our children grow up, to a large extent, as we shape them, for better or for worse. They are likely to go in the direction and pursue the trajectory that we trained them for. Thus, if we train up a son or daughter to know and love Jesus, there is a good chance he or she will. But this is not a guarantee.

Questions 7–10

Each small group member might pick a different proverb, and for various reasons. The key to the process of picking a proverb is to help small group members realize that these passages of Scripture are relevant and powerful. Once each group member adopts a proverb, it will become clear that there are many other lessons of wisdom to be learned from this powerful book of the Bible.

Solomon: Extreme Folly

THE HEART
of a Leader

In this small group study we will focus on how a person can move from wisdom to folly, and we will seek to identify ways to stop this process before we go too far. There are decisions that get made all along the way that can help or hinder us. There are steps we can take in our journey of faith that have the potential to ruin even the best of people and lead them into the depths of folly. Take time to search your heart as you prepare to lead this study. Prepare to hear God speak to you about where your heart needs to come back in line with God's will for your life.

THE PRAYER
of a Leader

As a leader, you have the opportunity to study this lesson in advance and see if you have begun walking on the road to foolishness. Take time to reflect on each of the four detours Solomon took and ask God to help you see if you are headed toward wisdom or folly. If you see areas where wisdom is growing in your life, thank God for this and pray for the power to stay on the right path. If the Holy Spirit alerts you to ways you are walking the path of foolishness, seek to repent and turn from these ways. Even the wisest of people can be enticed to walk in the way of fools. Let this be an opportunity for you to make sure your feet are on the right path.

Questions 2–4

In 1 Kings 11 we see Solomon at the end of his life. Rather than a celebration of his wisdom, we read a chronicle of his foolish choices and how these choices impacted those around him. Some of the most chilling words about Solomon are found in 1 Kings 11:4–6:

> As Solomon grew old, his wives turned his heart after other gods, and his heart was not fully devoted to the LORD his God, as the heart of David his father had been. He followed Ashtoreth the goddess of the Sidonians, and Molech the detestable god of the Ammonites. So Solomon did evil in the eyes of the LORD; he did not follow the LORD completely, as David his father had done.

LEADER'S NOTES

How did Solomon go from extreme wisdom to such blatant disobedience in a few brief chapters? In these verses we learn that Solomon followed Ashtoreth, a Canaanite fertility goddess. This false deity was closely connected to cultic temple prostitution that degraded people and greatly offended God. We also read that Solomon followed Molech, the "detestable" god of the Ammonite people. Molech was another false god, but there was a particularly hideous aspect to Molech worship, namely, human sacrifices. The Ammonites and others who followed Molech were known to sacrifice their infants to Molech on his altar.

Israel was commanded to have nothing to do with the high places except to destroy them. However, with some regularity, instead of demolishing these high places, especially before the temple was constructed, Israel converted some of them and began worshiping God there.

They tried to fit in with the religious culture of that day. People from the nation of Israel went to these pagan high places, but instead of worshiping idols, they tried to worship the one true God. They meant well. They had good intentions. And God didn't strike them down. In fact, sometimes, confusing as it may be, in his mercy, God even met them there.

It is important that all followers of Christ understand what was happening when the people of Israel tried to adopt these pagan places of worship. Even though they had good intentions, even though God didn't punish them immediately, they were *still not fully obedient*. Good intentions are never a substitute for obedience. The people were not separating themselves totally from pagan idolatry. God had commanded them to have nothing to do with these high places, but they decided to dabble a little bit. They allowed just a little wiggle room, and it cost them dearly.

Questions 5–6

Solomon began with a little wiggle room himself. Before long, he was rewriting the rule book. Take note of how many ways Solomon began to break God's clear commands. In each of these areas Solomon may have felt that God's rules were good and should be obeyed. But somehow, they just did not seem to apply to him and his situation.

Look closely at some of the detailed and specific commands God gave in Deuteronomy 17:16–17 to those who were to rule over his people:

> The king, moreover, must not acquire great numbers of horses for himself or make the people return to Egypt to get more of them, for the LORD has told you, "You are not to go back that way again." He must not take many wives, or his heart will be led astray. He must not accumulate large amounts of silver and gold.

It seems pretty clear:

1. no horses from Egypt
2. not too many wives
3. no large amounts of wealth

Yet Solomon did not think all of these commands applied to him. Just look at what transpired in his life. The specific commands given three centuries earlier were all broken by Solomon. When these are listed in 1 Kings 10:23–11:13, they show up in essentially the same order as they were given in Deuteronomy. What an indictment of Solomon's rebellious heart!

God commanded the kings of Israel to stay away from any arms build-up that would give them the tendency to rely on their own power and not on God. Yet one of the first things Solomon did was strike a treaty with the king of Egypt. He married an Egyptian wife, and he bought twelve thousand horses, most of them from Egypt. Strike one! God told the kings to avoid amassing wealth. He wanted them to rely on his provision, not their own stockpile. Yet Solomon made silver as common as rocks in the street. Strike two! God said to avoid having too many wives, and Solomon went on to set a world record with seven hundred wives. A big strike three!

Questions 7–8

When we read the end of 1 Kings 11:2, we come across one of the saddest words recorded about Solomon's life—the word "nevertheless." This word jumps off the page as we read it and see what follows. Solomon's "nevertheless" attitude and actions led to his downfall.

> *Nevertheless, Solomon held fast to them in love. He had seven hundred wives of royal birth and three hundred concubines, and his wives led him astray. As Solomon grew old, his wives turned his heart after other gods, and his heart was not fully devoted to the LORD his God, as the heart of David his father had been. He followed Ashtoreth the goddess of the Sidonians, and Molech the detestable god of the Ammonites. So Solomon did evil in the eyes of the LORD; he did not follow the LORD completely, as David his father had done. (1 Kings 11:2–6)*

Solomon knew what he was doing was wrong. This wasn't just a little rule about some gold and horses from Egypt. God had made it crystal clear that his people were to avoid those who worshiped false gods and idols. God warned them that unbelieving spouses could become a snare to them. Sadly, that is exactly what happened in Solomon's life.

Questions 9–10

In 1 Kings 9:1–2 Solomon had completed one of the high points in his life and career. He had finished and dedicated the temple. We read that God appeared to him again:

> *When Solomon had finished building the temple of the Lord and the royal palace, and had achieved all he had desired to do, the Lord appeared to him a second time, as he had appeared to him at Gibeon.*

It was at Gibeon (1 Kings 3:5) that God had appeared to Solomon and invited him to ask for whatever he wanted. Do you remember what Solomon asked of God? For wisdom! That was all. Since then, Solomon had become a very different man.

Now, when God appears again to Solomon at Gibeon, he comes with a warning. In effect God says, "If you follow me, I will bless you. But if you refuse to follow me, I will cut you off!" God knew the condition of Solomon's life and heart, and it was time for a firm warning. Solomon was on a crash course to disaster, so God stepped in with a warning.

Our hearts should be open to correction. We must humbly listen when God speaks and calls us to change. Our defense mechanisms can be turned up so high that we have a hard time hearing corrective words from God or his servants. But we need to resist this tendency and learn to soften our hearts and open our ears.

Job: Where Is God When It Hurts?

THE HEART
of a Leader

The hard truth is that everybody will spend some time in the land of Uz. Some people are living there right now. Others have just traveled through and still feel the aftermath. Still others don't know it, but the land of Uz is directly ahead. For all of us, knowing God in his creative beauty and awesome power is one of the greatest gifts we can have when we travel through the land of Uz.

THE PRAYER
of a Leader

Job is an absolutely remarkable book. Studying it invariably involves a steep learning curve for anyone who really digs in. As you prepare to lead this small group, get ready to meet with God. Specifically, take time to read Job 38–41 and reflect on the questions God asks Job. Listen to these words as if they were written to you. Then prepare for your small group with a heart saturated with the reality of who God is and what he has done. Celebrate God's goodness and pray for the Spirit to meet your small group and speak to each heart.

Questions 2–4

As we study Job, it may help to compare it to a play. It is written much that way. Think of a play in which there are two stages. There is an upper stage, which is built high on risers and is near the ceiling of the theater. On that stage is the activity that takes place in heaven. Those on the upper stage can look down and see what is happening on the stage below. Then there is a lower stage, which features the activity taking place on earth. Those on the lower stage can't see what is happening above them on the upper stage.

We, the readers (those watching the drama unfold), are able to see what's happening on both stages—upper and lower. This is crucial to the story. We know what's going on in both settings. We must remember that the characters on earth (the lower stage) do not have our vantage point. They are aware of the activity around them but not above them. They know nothing about what's happening on the higher stage. They have a limited perspective.

In the beginning of Job, we discover that Satan appears on the upper stage, in heaven, but then he moves to the lower stage. When he does, Job loses everything. He is pummeled with loss, pain, and heartache. Job's livestock, wealth, servants, and children are all swept away.

When this happens, we see Job's response (Job 1:20–22):

> *At this, Job got up and tore his robe and shaved his head. Then he fell to the ground in worship and said:*
>
> > *"Naked I came from my mother's womb,*
> > *and naked I will depart.*
> > *The LORD gave and the LORD has taken away;*
> > *may the name of the LORD be praised."*
>
> *In all this, Job did not sin by charging God with wrongdoing.*

We also learn that Job grieves and expresses it in outward ways that were common in his day. He tore his clothing and shaved his head. Moreover, Job falls to the ground in worship and speaks words of blessing and praise. Job's response is both sorrow and worship.

In Job 2 we switch back to the upper stage. God says to Satan:

> *Have you considered my servant Job? There is no one on earth like him; he is blameless and upright, a man who fears God and shuns evil. And he still maintains his integrity, though you incited me against him to ruin him without any reason. (2:3)*

Satan responds that the only reason Job maintains his integrity is that God has treated him well. If God allowed his body to be touched with pain, he would certainly curse God.

From this point on, the action of this drama takes place on the lower stage. It is critical that we clarify what is going on in heaven. At first glance the action in heaven looks strange and confusing. It appears as if a cosmic wager between God and Satan is taking place. It can seem as if God is using Job and his family as pawns to win a bet or prove a point to Satan.

This is not what is going on at all. The key question on the upper stage and in the whole book is, "Does Job fear God for nothing?" Satan is saying: "Job is devoted to you and worships you because it's in his self-interest to do it. You scratch his back. He scratches yours. It's a quid pro quo." Satan is charging God with being naïve.

After losing all his possessions and his children, Job gets hit with a second wave of suffering. His body is afflicted with pain most of us can't even imagine. This time his response is different. He does *not* fall to the ground and worship. He does *not* say, "May the name of the LORD be praised."

Rather, this time Job sits on an ash heap. Maybe he's grieving. Maybe he's isolated, because people are afraid he has leprosy. His wife speaks for the first and last time in this drama, saying simply: "Are you still holding on to your integrity? Curse God and die!" (2:9).

Job's response (2:10) shows that he is struggling to understand God: "You are talking like a foolish woman. Shall we accept good from God, and not trouble?" The words "and not trouble" can be translated "and not evil." Job is struggling to understand if God is the kind of person who sends evil. Is God really good? That is the question on the lower stage.

This text goes on to say: "In all this, Job did not sin in what he said." This is a hint of what is going on inside Job. After the first wave of suffering Job faced, we are told that "in all this, Job did not sin by charging God with wrongdoing." Now, after this wave of suffering, there's a little qualification: "Job did not sin in what he said." Job has begun to struggle in his heart. He is not expressing it in words, yet.

Questions 5–7

Job's friends plan to sit next to him and take on his anguish. When they saw Job, they could hardly recognize him. They had heard it was bad, but nothing could prepare them for what they saw when they met Job.

Usually when we visit somebody who is sick or in a bad condition, we try to cheer them up. Have you ever been so sick that when someone came to visit you, they took one look and burst into tears? That's what happened to Job. It was so awful that all they could do was weep. Then, they did something remarkable. They just sat with him for seven days and seven nights. They did not say a word. They were with him in silence.

In his pain, Job spews so much venom that his three friends can't stand it. They can't listen to it. Finally they respond. And most of the book of Job is a series of speeches given by Job along with the responses of his friends. We can't look at all of the speeches, but we can identify the key theme that each of Job's friends brought forth.

Eliphaz argued that the innocent don't perish and the upright are not destroyed. In effect, he is saying that the innocent do not suffer.

> *Consider now: Who, being innocent, has ever perished?*
> *Where were the upright ever destroyed?* (4:7)

Bildad gets a little more direct. He says that Job's children died because of their sin. They had it coming. His theory is that our suffering is a result of personal sin and rebellion.

> *When your children sinned against him,*
>> *he gave them over to the penalty of their sin. (8:4)*

Zophar suggests that Job's suffering is a result of his personal sin. He calls Job to repent and turn from his sin.

> *Yet if you devote your heart to him*
>> *and stretch out your hands to him,*
> *if you put away the sin that is in your hand*
>> *and allow no evil to dwell in your tent,*
> *then you will lift up your face without shame;*
>> *you will stand firm and without fear. (11:13–15)*

In each case, when Job's friends put forth their theory, Job counters with his argument and defense. At one point Job gets testy and somewhat sarcastic: "Doubtless you are the people, and wisdom will die with you!" (12:2). It is important that we hear Job's three friends giving voice to one central idea, namely, that pain, suffering, and sorrow in this life are a direct consequence for personal sin.

Questions 8–10

All through chapters 38–41 we see God delighting in his creation. Even creatures that are of no apparent and no strategic value are a joy to him. God doesn't get anything from them, but he still loves them. A quick survey will make this very clear:

- *The ostrich* (39:13–18). This is just a wonderful, fun passage. The ostrich is a goofy-looking animal. God says that she flaps her wings joyfully—as if she thinks that's going to get her somewhere. She's not a great mom. She lays her eggs but can't even remember where she left them.
- *The hippo* (40:15–19). In the ancient world, the behemoth was considered what they called the chaos monster. Some people wrote that it had to be eliminated for the earth to be habitable for human beings. But that's not God's opinion. God ranks this strange creature as a great success among his works.

• *The wild ox, the donkey, and other animals.* You can't miss God's joy and celebration of his creation.

By the end of the story, Job finds out the kind of person God is, and that's enough for him. The hinge—the resolution of this whole book—is in 42:5–6. Job is speaking to God:

> *My ears had heard of you*
> > *but now my eyes have seen you.*
> *Therefore I despise myself*
> > *and repent in dust and ashes.*

This is enough for Job. He has heard, he has seen, he is satisfied! When Job says that he repents in dust and ashes, he is not saying, "I will now live with low self-esteem." This is a Hebrew way of saying he is entering into a new strategy for living. He is saying to God, "I can trust you." We can almost hear Job declare, "I can trust you with my children; I know that they are better off in your hands now. I can trust you with my pain; I know that you will redeem every bit of it. You are the kind of God who treasures and cares for everything. I place my full trust in you."

LEADER'S NOTES

The Divided Kingdom: What Puts Community at Risk

LEADER'S NOTES

THE HEART
of a Leader

In this session we will identify four factors that put community at risk. Take time, before you lead this session, to examine your heart and life. Do any of these community-breaking patterns exist in your life? Do you need to change a life pattern or attitude for the sake of becoming more of a community builder? Take time to ask God to shape you into a follower of Christ who blesses and builds community.

THE PRAYER
of a Leader

We live in a world of brokenness. Broken marriages, families, churches, friendships, business deals, and hearts are common. In light of this reality, take time to pray for your small group members in any area of their lives where they are facing brokenness. Pray for the Holy Spirit to meet you in this small group study and help each member of your group grow in a hunger and desire for unity and community to rule in their life.

Question 1
This question can be a delicate one in some churches. While you should encourage group members to talk, try not to allow the discussion to degenerate into an all-out gripe session that destroys community.

HISTORICAL CONTEXT: A BASIC TIMELINE
Before we look at the community risk factors, we should look at some introductory information about this section of the Bible. It's important, first of all, to understand that the kingdom period of ancient Israel lasted about five hundred years—from 1050 to 586 B.C. This period of history can be broken into four distinct phases. The first phase was the *United Kingdom Period* under Kings Saul, David, and Solomon. This lasted 120 years.

Next was the *Divided Kingdom Period*. This is when civil war broke out between Israel and Judah. During this time, ten tribes of Israel formed the northern kingdom, with Samaria as its capital and Jeroboam as its king. Two tribes formed the southern kingdom, with Jerusalem as its capital and

Rehoboam as its king. This phase lasted about two hundred years until the Assyrian Empire came and invaded Israel, the northern kingdom.

In 722 B.C. the northern kingdom (Israel) was attacked, destroyed, and dispersed to the four corners of the ancient world. This marked the beginning of phase three—the *Surviving Kingdom Period* of the southern kingdom (Judah). For about 136 years Judah survived, but then the Babylonians came and invaded. They destroyed Jerusalem and took many of the people to Babylonia as exiles for seventy years.

This exile marked the fourth phase of the kingdom—the *Dissolved Kingdom Period*. Israel, the northern kingdom, has been gone for generations. Now Judah, the southern kingdom, was exiled to a foreign land. They were prisoners of war. At this point, the kingdom was dissolved. Although a remnant came back to the land under the leadership of Zerubbabel and later Ezra and Nehemiah, the history of God's people as a nation with a human king was over.

Questions 2–4

One of the defining moments for the community of ancient Israel came when Rehoboam succeeded Solomon, his father, as king. At his inauguration, when the leaders of the twelve tribes of Israel came to crown their new king, he had an opportunity to build community—to strengthen community. Instead, he blew it up.

When the elders of the twelve tribes came to the inauguration of Rehoboam, they had one request: "Your father put a heavy yoke on us, but now lighten the harsh labor and the heavy yoke he put on us, and we will serve you" (1Kings 12:5). Rehoboam said, "Give me three days to think about it." Then he got counsel from the elders who had served his father during his lifetime. When he asked them what he should do, they said: "If today you will be a servant to these people and serve them and give them a favorable answer, they will always be your servants" (1 Kings 12:7).

But Rehoboam rejected the advice the elders gave him and instead consulted the young men he had grown up with. Their advice was very different: "Tell these people who have said to you, 'Your father put a heavy yoke on us, but make our yoke lighter'—tell them, 'My little finger is thicker than my father's waist. My father laid on you a heavy yoke; I will make it even heavier. My father scourged you with whips; I will scourge you with scorpions'" (1 Kings 12:10–11).

Rehoboam refused the path of service. Instead, he decided to rule with an iron fist, and it cost him the unity of the kingdom. Over a century of the twelve tribes being united ended when Rehoboam declared that he would not be a servant leader. He abused his position. He didn't listen to wise counsel. He was more concerned about himself than his people, and he put the community of Israel into a tailspin from which they never recovered. It was a defining moment in his life and in the history of Israel.

In the same way, leaders today consign their churches, businesses, families, and any group of people to disunity when they refuse to be servant leaders. Every leader faces the same defining moment Rehoboam encountered. Will I serve or demand that I be served? Will I build community or destroy it?

Questions 5–6

Although the kingdom was divided politically, with Rehoboam as king in the south and Jeroboam as the king in the north, they were still united spiritually. All of the Israelites in both kingdoms were still expected to make a pilgrimage several times a year to Jerusalem to worship God. Jerusalem was still the location of the temple and the center of the religious life of all Israelites. It also happened to be the capital of the southern kingdom and the place where Rehoboam ruled. All of this caused a problem for Jeroboam, the king of Israel. He articulates his concern in 1 Kings 12:26–27:

> Jeroboam thought to himself, "The kingdom will now likely revert to the house of David. If these people go up to offer sacrifices at the temple of the LORD in Jerusalem, they will again give their allegiance to their lord, Rehoboam king of Judah. They will kill me and return to King Rehoboam."

Jeroboam was filled with fear because he knew his kingship would always be in jeopardy as long as the people under his rule went to the capital of the southern kingdom to worship. Thus, he came up with a solution. He made two golden calves and set up his own places of worship. Jeroboam established a formal system of idolatry, which was clearly forbidden. Then, in an effort to sway the people of Israel away from Jerusalem and toward his new places of worship, he said: "It is too much for you to go up to Jerusalem. Here are your gods, O Israel, who brought you up out of Egypt" (1 Kings 12:28).

Nothing can get a biblically functioning community going down the wrong path faster than individuals who manipulate spiritual language for personal agenda. That was the sin of Jeroboam. He made idols out of his own political agenda. Then he manipulated people into following his false gods. We must be careful when people use spiritual language in dogmatic tones. It puts a community at risk.

Some people come to us saying things like:

- "God spoke to me and told me you should. . . ."
- "God told me his plan for you is. . . ."
- "God showed me that our church has to. . . ."
- "Pastor, I have a word for you from God! He said. . . ."

They may be sincere. They may actually have a word from God for us. But they may also be trying to manipulate us. We must approach this topic with a double caution. First, we must be aware that God does speak, and we need to hear when others have received a word from God. We must take care not to miss when God is speaking to us or his church. The second warning, and one that applies to the passage we are studying, is that we must be careful when people are using spiritual language to forward their own selfish agenda. This happened in Jeroboam's day, and it still happens today.

Questions 7–8

Abijah became the king of Judah after Rehoboam. When we read of his life and how God evaluated him, we are struck by these words: " He committed all the sins his father had done before him; his heart was not fully devoted to the LORD his God, as the heart of David his forefather had been" (1 Kings 15:3).

The sin of halfheartedness repeats itself over and over again during the history of the kings. Abijah was a king who did not follow God with his whole heart. He soon discovered that following God halfheartedly was not only foolish; it was dangerous. The problem with a heart that is only half full of God is that it is half empty! This leaves room for other affections to move in and crowd God out. It opens the door for idolatry, which is exactly what crept into Abijah's heart, just as it had entered the heart of his father. When our hearts are only half full of God, we become vulnerable to temptation, sin, and all kinds of evil. A heart that is not fully devoted to God quickly becomes a heart that wanders away.

Questions 9–10

Asa, the king of Judah, ruled for forty-one years. He started out so well. In 1 Kings 15:11 we read, "Asa did what was right in the eyes of the LORD, as his father David had done." When a superior army from Ethiopia came and invaded Judah, he called on God for help. God answered his prayer and gave him a great victory against overwhelming odds.

LEADER'S NOTES

For thirty-five years, Asa trusted and relied on God, and he experienced peace on his borders. There was no peace, however, within the divided kingdom because Asa and Baasha (king of Israel) were at war throughout their reigns.

Then, something happened in the thirty-sixth year of Asa's reign. The king of Israel took one of the border towns between Israel and Judah. When this happened, Asa stopped trusting in God. He turned away from God. Instead of relying on God to overcome his enemies, Asa turned to Ben-Hadad, king of Aram, for assistance. Asa actually robbed the gold and silver from the treasury of the temple in Jerusalem to pay this pagan king for help to protect him against his own kinsmen.

Then, when one of the prophets came and rebuked him for turning away from God and for making an unholy alliance with a foreign king, Asa responded in anger. He was so enraged that he put the prophet in prison and brutally oppressed some of the people. Asa's heart was so far from God that he would not hear or receive godly counsel. Within a couple years, Asa died a broken and defeated man. Yet even in his illness he did not seek help from the Lord.

Willow Creek Association
Vision, Training, Resources for Prevailing Churches

This resource was created to serve you and to help you in building a local church that prevails!

Since 1992, the Willow Creek Association (WCA) has been linking like-minded, action-oriented churches with each other and with strategic vision, training, and resources. Now a worldwide network of over 6,400 churches from more than ninety denominations, the WCA works to equip Member Churches and others with the tools needed to build prevailing churches. Our desire is to inspire, equip, and encourage Christian leaders to build biblically functioning churches that reach increasing numbers of unchurched people, not just with innovations from Willow Creek Community Church in South Barrington, Illinois, but from any church in the world that has experienced God-given breakthroughs.

WILLOW CREEK CONFERENCES

Each year, thousands of local church leaders, staff, and volunteers—from WCA Member Churches and others—attend one of our conferences or training events. Conferences offered on the Willow Creek campus in South Barrington, Illinois, include:

Prevailing Church Conference: Foundational training for staff and volunteers working to build a prevailing local church.

Prevailing Church Workshops: More than fifty strategic, day-long workshops covering seven topic areas that represent key characteristics of a prevailing church; offered twice each year.

Promiseland Conference: Children's ministries; infant through fifth grade.

Student Ministries Conference: Junior and senior high ministries.

Willow Creek Arts Conference: Vision and training for Christian artists using their gifts in the ministries of local churches.

Leadership Summit: Envisioning and equipping Christians with leadership gifts and responsibilities; broadcast live via satellite to eighteen cities across North America.

Contagious Evangelism Conference: Encouragement and training for churches and church leaders who want to be strategic in reaching lost people for Christ.

Small Groups Conference: Exploring how developing a church *of* small groups can play a vital role in developing authentic Christian community that leads to spiritual transformation.

To find out more about WCA conferences, visit our website at www.willowcreek.com.

PREVAILING CHURCH REGIONAL WORKSHOPS

Each year the WCA team leads several, two-day training events in select cities across the United States. Some twenty day-long workshops are offered in topic areas including leadership, next-generation ministries, small groups, arts and worship, evangelism, spiritual gifts, financial stewardship, and spiritual formation. These events make quality training more accessible and affordable to larger groups of staff and volunteers.

To find out more about Prevailing Church Regional Workshops, visit our website at www.willowcreek.com.

WILLOW CREEK RESOURCES™

Churches can look to Willow Creek Resources™ for a trusted channel of ministry tools in areas of leadership, evangelism, spiritual gifts, small groups, drama, contemporary music, financial stewardship, spiritual transformation, and more. For ordering information, call (800) 570-9812 or visit our website at www.willowcreek.com.

WCA MEMBERSHIP

Membership in the Willow Creek Association as well as attendance at WCA Conferences is for churches, ministries, and leaders who hold to a historic, orthodox understanding of biblical Christianity. The annual church membership fee of $249 provides substantial discounts for your entire team on all conferences and Willow Creek Resources, networking opportunities with other outreach-oriented churches, a bimonthly newsletter, a subscription to the *Defining Moments* monthly audio journal for leaders, and more.

To find out more about WCA membership, visit our website at www.willowcreek.com.

WILLOWNET (WWW.WILLOWCREEK.COM)

This Internet resource service provides access to hundreds of Willow Creek messages, drama scripts, songs, videos, and multimedia ideas. The system allows you to sort through these elements and download them for a fee.

Our website also provides detailed information on the Willow Creek Association, Willow Creek Community Church, WCA membership, conferences, training events, resources, and more.

WILLOWCHARTS.COM (WWW.WILLOWCHARTS.COM)

Designed for local church worship leaders and musicians, WillowCharts.com provides online access to hundreds of music charts and chart components, including choir, orchestral, and horn sections, as well as rehearsal tracks and video streaming of Willow Creek Community Church performances.

THE NET (HTTP://STUDENTMINISTRY.WILLOWCREEK.COM)

The NET is an online training and resource center designed by and for student ministry leaders. It provides an inside look at the structure, vision, and mission of prevailing student ministries from around the world. The NET gives leaders access to complete programming elements, including message outlines, dramas, small group questions, and more. An indispensable resource and networking tool for prevailing student ministry leaders!

CONTACT THE WILLOW CREEK ASSOCIATION

If you have comments or questions, or would like to find out more about WCA events or resources, please contact us:

Willow Creek Association
P.O. Box 3188, Barrington, IL 60011-3188
Phone: (800) 570-9812 or (847) 765-0070
Fax: (888) 922-0035 or (847) 765-5046
Web: www.willowcreek.com

Creating a New Community: Life-Changing Stories from the Pentateuch

Old Testament Challenge

Discover the Life-Changing Relevance
of the Old Testament

John Ortberg with Kevin and Sherry Harney

This dynamic program takes your church on an eye-opening, heart-searching journey through Scripture on three interlocking levels:

- **Whole congregation**—The major themes of the Old Testament snap into focus during 32 weeks of creative and powerful messages that take your entire congregation through the Old Testament.
- **Small groups**—Truths taught in corporate worship get reinforced through discussion and relationship. Small groups dig deeper into God's Word and apply it to their daily lives.
- **Individual**—The Scriptures get up-close-and-personal as each participant is challenged through the *Taking the Old Testament Challenge* individual reading guide.

This threefold approach will drive the truths of Scripture deep into the heart and life of each participant, with applications designed to turn lessons into lifestyles and principles into practice.

From the beginning to the end of our lives, we hunger for community. It's not just how we were created—it's why! God, who enjoys relationship within his being as Father, Son, and Holy Spirit, designed us to reflect his nature through loving and life-giving relationship with him and with each other. Only by participating in God's plan for community can the longing of our hearts be satisfied.

These nine interweaving messages, small group studies, and personal study assignments search the Pentateuch to reveal God's passionate desire for intimacy with his people and among his people. Volume one of the Old Testament Challenge educates through action, not just words. It's an exciting new approach for helping the people in your church move closer to God and to each other.

Old Testament Challenge Vol. 1 kit includes:
- Nine messages by John Ortberg on audio CDs
- Church Teacher Resource Book with materials for nine OTC messages
- DVD and VHS Video presenting an OTC "vision-casting" message by John Ortberg and four creative video elements for use during OTC messages
- Small Group Discussion Guide with nine lessons that follow the OTC sermons
- CD-ROM providing nine Power Point® presentations for use with each OTC message, Ten FAQ resources for the first ten weeks of the OTC reading guide, and several units of a game, Are You an Old Testament Expert?
- *Taking the Old Testament Challenge* reading guide with a forty week (and optional thirty-two week) reading plan.
- *Implementation Guide* for Old Testament Challenge

All materials except audio sermons by John Ortberg also sold separately.

Curriculum Kit: 0-310-24891-4

DVD Video: 0-310-25242-3

VHS Video: 0-310-25243-1

Small Group Discussion Guide: 0-310-24893-0

Teaching Guide: 0-310-24892-2

PowerPoint® CD-ROM: 0-310-25244-X

Taking the Old Testament Challenge: 0-310-24913-9

Implementation Guide: 0-310-24939-2

Stepping Out in Faith: Life-Changing Examples from the History of Israel

Old Testament Challenge

Discover the Life-Changing Relevance
of the Old Testament

John Ortberg with Kevin and Sherry Harney

This dynamic program takes your church on an eye-opening, heart-searching journey through Scripture on three interlocking levels:

- **Whole congregation**—The major themes of the Old Testament snap into focus during 32 weeks of creative and powerful messages that take your entire congregation through the Old Testament.
- **Small groups**—Truths taught in corporate worship get reinforced through discussion and relationship. Small groups dig deeper into God's Word and apply it to their daily lives.
- **Individual**—The Scriptures get up-close-and-personal as each participant is challenged through the *Taking the Old Testament Challenge* individual reading guide.

As we look closely at the highs and lows of Israel's history, we will discover lessons that can transform and shape both our present and our future. These seven interweaving messages, small group studies, and personal study assignments search the history of Israel and reveal God's presence with his people as they follow him on an amazing journey of faith. Volume two of the Old Testament Challenge educates through action, not just words.

Old Testament Challenge Vol. 2 kit includes:
- Seven messages by John Ortberg on audio CDs
- Church Teaching Guide with materials for seven Old Testament Challenge messages
- Small Group Discussion Guide with seven lessons that follow the OTC sermons
- DVD and VHS Video presenting an OTC "vision-casting" message by John Ortberg and three creative elements for use during OTC messages
- CD-ROM containing seven PowerPoint® slides for use with each OTC message, ten FAQ resources for the second ten weeks of the OTC reading guide, and several units of the game, "Are You an Old Testament Expert?"

All materials except audio sermons by John Ortberg also sold separately.

Curriculum Kit: 0-310-24931-7
DVD Video: 0-310-24935-X
VHS Video: 0-310-25253-9

Small Group Discussion Guide: 0-310-24933-3
Teaching Guide: 0-310-24932-5
PowerPoint® CD-ROM: 0-310-24936-8

**Developing a Heart for God: Life-Changing
Lessons from the Wisdom Books**

Old Testament Challenge

Discover the Life-Changing Relevance
of the Old Testament

*John Ortberg with Kevin
and Sherry Harney*

This dynamic program takes your church on an eye-opening, heart-searching journey through Scripture on three interlocking levels:

- **Whole congregation**—The major themes of the Old Testament snap into
  focus during 32 weeks of creative and powerful messages that take your
  entire congregation through the Old Testament.
- **Small groups**—Truths taught in corporate worship get reinforced through
  discussion and relationship. Small groups dig deeper into God's Word and
  apply it to their daily lives.
- **Individual**—The Scriptures get up-close-and-personal as each participant
  is challenged through the Taking the Old Testament Challenge individual
  reading guide.

This threefold approach will drive the truths of Scripture deep into the heart and
life of each participant, with applications designed to turn lessons into lifestyles
and principles into practice.

Developing a Heart for God: Life-Changing Lessons from the Wisdom Books is
the third kit in this series and contains everything you need to preach eight sermons
or teach eight sessions as well as lead eight small group discussions.

Old Testament Challenge Vol. 3 kit includes:
- Eight messages by John Ortberg on audio CDs
- Church Teaching Guide with materials for eight Old Testament Challenge
  messages
- Small Group Discussion Guide following the eight OTC sermons for weekly
  or biweekly use, featuring leader's notes in the back of each guide
- DVD and VHS Video presenting an OTC "vision-casting" message by John
  Ortberg and creative elements for use during OTC messages
- CD-ROM containing eight PowerPoint® slides for each teaching session,
  ten FAQ resources for the third ten weeks of the OTC reading guide, and
  several units of a game, Are You an Old Testament Expert?

All materials except audio sermons by John Ortberg also sold separately.

Curriculum Kit: 0-310-25031-5
DVD Video: 0-310-25035-8
VHS Video: 0-310-25263-6

Small Group Discussion Guide: 0-310-25033-1
Teaching Guide: 0-310-25032-3
PowerPoint® CD-ROM: 0-310-25036-6

AN A–Z TOUR
OLD TESTAMENT CHALLENGE

Implementation Guide
Discover the Life-Changing Relevance
of the Old Testament

Kevin Harney and
Mindy Caliguire

The *Implementation Guide* gives aid on how to
lead a comprehensive tour through the Old
Testament Challenge experience. It is an A–Z overview of the full program, giving
leaders all the tools they will need to rally church support, build a leadership team,
prepare for the Old Testament Challenge, launch the OTC, lead the thirty-two-
week Old Testament program on three interlocking levels (congregation wide, small
groups, and individual), and end the Old Testament Challenge in a way that will
propel church members forward with a new passion and commitment to God's
Word. Through using this guide, the Old Testament Challenge will be an experience your congregation will never forget.

> *The OTC offers a great benefit to those who take the challenge. At our
> church, we often found that people suffered from "spiritual information
> overload." They would hear one talk at a weekend service, another during
> our mid-week worship time; they would discuss a third topic in their small
> group and look at a fourth one in their personal reading. It was like drink-
> ing from a fire hydrant. The OTC has a revolutionary impact on spiritual
> growth because it weds together a teaching experience, small group learning,
> and individual study all around one weekly theme! This guide will give you a
> road map to lead your congregation on a life-transforming journey through
> the Old Testament.*
>
> – John Ortberg

Softcover: 0-310-24939-2

Pick up a copy today at your favorite bookstore!

ZONDERVAN™

GRAND RAPIDS, MICHIGAN 49530 USA

WWW.ZONDERVAN.COM

WILLOW
Willow Creek Resources

We want to hear from you. Please send your comments about this book to us in care of zreview@zondervan.com. Thank you.

ZONDERVAN™

GRAND RAPIDS, MICHIGAN 49530 USA

WWW.ZONDERVAN.COM